# Chanakya
# in You

# Chanakya in You

## Adventures of a Modern Kingmaker

**NATIONAL BESTSELLER**

Radhakrishnan Pillai

JAICO PUBLISHING HOUSE

Ahmedabad  Bangalore  Bhopal  Bhubaneswar  Chennai
Delhi  Hyderabad  Kolkata  Lucknow  Mumbai

Published by Jaico Publishing House
A-2 Jash Chambers, 7-A Sir Phirozshah Mehta Road
Fort, Mumbai - 400 001
jaicopub@jaicobooks.com
www.jaicobooks.com

CHANAKYA IN YOU
ISBN 978-81-8495-660-3

First Jaico Impression: 2015
Sixteenth Jaico Impression: 2018

Page design and layout: R Ajith Kumar, Delhi

Printed by
Snehesh Printers
320-A, Shah & Nahar Ind. Est. A-1
Lower Parel, Mumbai - 400 013

*To all my readers who have inspired me to write this book.*

# 1

# Grandpa's Advice

I once had a very loving grandpa...

I guess all grandpas are loving. But the bond I shared with my grandpa was different. First of all, I had only ever known one grandpa in my life – the father of my father. Also, I was brought up in a metropolitan city, while my grandparents lived in a village.

So, every vacation I looked forward to visiting them. It was a special event for both me and my grandparents. They waited eagerly for their grandchildren to come home and spend time with them. As a child I knew that with them around me, no one in this entire world would dare object to my pranks... not even my own parents. I had full freedom to do whatever I wanted!

There is a saying, "Why are grandparents and grandchildren close to each other?" "Because they have a common enemy in between..."

So, the bond between these two generations is very unique. While you are a parent, you are burdened with so many responsibilities, that it is difficult to dedicate enough quality time to your kids even though you really want to.

As for our grandparents, since they have all the time in the world, they need someone to pass on their love and experience to. They find life's fulfillment in their grandchildren. And the kids in turn look forward to receiving their wisdom in the form of stories, long walks in the gardens, fields and market places.

My grandpa was a master storyteller; he had so much to tell us. While many of these stories were from his own life, most of them were from the lives of others. He would lead us to his library, which was full of books, while grandma was busy in the kitchen preparing a variety of delicacies for everyone.

At the time, my cousins and I were not really interested in the books he held so dear, yet his library was amazing. It was his private den, with neatly arranged books classified and categorized and each covered and neatly labeled. He even showed us a register, where he maintained a list of the type of books he had: from science to world literature, and poems to paintings, he had books spanning a wide range of interests. But I was far more interested in listening to his stories than reading those, heavy, wordy books. Besides, grandpa had a knack for recalling events from different books he had read and weaving them into stories that we as kids could understand.

One of my senior cousins, who was very studious, once asked him, "Grandpa, what is more important: reading books or listening to stories?"

"Both!" he said with great enthusiasm. "Not everybody has the interest and patience to read books, but everyone likes to listen to stories. And you will find that when you pay attention to the story, you will never be the same person again. But given that you" he pointed to all of us sitting around him, "are fortunate to go to school, you must make the effort to actually read books."

It felt like grandpa had conveyed a message to me. We were the lucky few who were blessed with good education and so, we should read books. There are many children in the world, who do not have the privilege to go to school and therefore cannot read or write. Instead, their only path to wisdom is through the tradition of story-telling. And so, from that day on, I decided to put my efforts into reading books, the very habit grandpa had cultivated all his life.

That evening, we were to be taken to the market along with my grandma, uncles and aunts. We looked forward to the outing as we knew we would be treated to some delicious roadside snacks. But for some reason, I did not feel like going out; I just wanted to spend time with grandpa.

When all my cousins had left, I hurried to the library to find my grandpa. He was sitting in his chair, engrossed in some books spread on the table. When he looked up, he was surprised to see me standing all alone.

"Why did you not go to the market?"

I quietly said, "Grandpa, I want to see your books!"

He had a smile on his face as if to say, "Okay, my dear little one, welcome to the world of books!"

Over the next one hour, he took me through every rack he had organized. He opened some of the books he held so dear and showed me the notes contained in each one of them.

What really attracted me was the number of books he had on ancient Indian wisdom. He had everything from the *Ramayana*, *Mahabharata*, and the *Upanishads* to the fables of *Panchatantra*. I realized then where he got all his stories from.

Suddenly, a question hit me and I asked him "Which of these books is your favourite, grandpa?"

"Kautilya's *Arthashastra*," he replied instantaneously.

What is that? I wondered.

Reading my mind, grandpa picked up the book and led me back to his table.

"Kautilya was also known as Chanakya."

Soon, a new world of stories began unfolding before me…

# 2

# The History of India

The loud, excited voices in the distance announced my cousins' arrival home. They all rushed into grandpa's study with two intentions: to let grandpa know they were ready for more stories, and to make me feel jealous that I had missed all the fun they had at the market. But my cousins had no idea that I had only gained by remaining home with my grandpa. I will forever treasure those special moments with him.

Once again, we sat down around grandpa to hear his next story. For my cousins, it was a new story, but for me, it was to understand what Kautilya's *Arthashastra* was.

Grandpa had a fascinating way of building up the story before he came to the point. We could visualize the events as though they were unravelling before our very eyes and we were a living part of that moment. He had the amazing ability to spark our imagination.

"The history of India is very unique," he began. "It is rich and vast. It is about the huge monuments such as forts, palaces and temples; it is about personalities, like kings and saints; it is about literature that describes various subjects, ranging from science to art. But most importantly, our history is about spirituality."

"Spirituality?" one of my cousins asked.

"Yes. Spirituality is man's search for God; the search for the meaning of life. It is a journey from being ordinary to becoming extraordinary, to discover your huge inner potential and the ability to achieve the impossible. Yet, spirituality is about overcoming your ego."

He was describing the essence of Indian history in a few, yet profound words.

"Where can we find spirituality in India?" asked a curious cousin of mine.

"Everywhere. It's all over. You can see it in the temples and other places of worship, in our homes and in the streets. You can see it in the idols you worship or in the quiet meditative state of your mind. It is the very essence of our culture."

I was a bit confused. These were abstract concepts and I could not understand what grandpa was trying to tell us. Maybe I was too young to relate to what he was saying; maybe I would have to wait until I grew up to understand exactly what grandpa meant. I guessed one needed to reach a certain level of maturity to understand spirituality.

I asked him, "Grandpa, when I grow up, will I become mature?'

He smiled and said, "It is when you mature, that you really grow up. Maturity is not about age, it comes with an understanding of life. There are many people who are ripe in their old age, yet they are immature in their approach towards life. On the other hand, certain children are very mature through responsible actions.

In fact, many of our saints were very young when they guided their generations. Dyaneshwar Maharaj, Adi Shankaracharya, Swami Vivekananda – these saints left their body very young, yet guided old men and women. There are many examples of the *Guru-Shishya* relationship, where the *Guru*, the teacher, was younger than the student."

"The teacher was younger than the student?" Very nice, I smiled to myself and said, "If I become mature soon, I can teach a few lessons to my school teacher too."

Intrigued, my cousins and I asked in unison, "Grandpa, how does one become mature?"

"There are many ways, but one of the easiest ways is to study history. History is full of experiences of people who have walked on this earth before you. It is about events, stories and incidents that your forefathers went through. It tells you about the way civilizations survived the test of time. It also tells you about mistakes our forefathers have made. And most importantly, it tells your stories as well. That's why it is called HIS-STORY."

I was not a good history student in school, but I loved how Grandpa made it very interesting. "Grandpa, I do not like history, because I cannot remember those dates. It's very difficult for me."

He smiled, "Yes, I understand. Sometimes dates are very confusing, but the history I am talking about is not just about remembering dates of certain events that you have to write down in exams. The history I am talking about is, not repeating the mistakes others made.

There are three types of people in this world. The first type learns by making mistakes; the second type keeps making mistakes but never learns; and finally, the third is the most intelligent type – they learn from the mistakes of others.

If you are smart, you will realize that you do not have to re-invent the wheel. You can be successful from the very beginning itself. What took generations to achieve, you can achieve in a few years. That is the power of knowledge, transferred from one generation to another in the form of books."

I was mentally transported to a different world, but woke up with a jolt the moment I heard the word 'books'. As though trying to take control of the discussion, I shouted, "Grandpa! You were talking about Kautilya's *Arthashastra*."

Initially, I was angry with my cousins. Grandpa was just beginning to tell me about it when they had already returned from the market place and amidst all the chaos, Grandpa digressed. But now, it seemed to me that we were finally back on track. I wanted to know more about Kautilya.

"Kautilya lived in the 4th century BC..."

History was just opening up a new chapter for me...

# 3

# The Kingmaker

"He was known by three names." There was a story behind each name and grandpa had studied them all in detail.

"Vishnugupta, Kautilya and Chanakya."

"He was first known as Vishnugupta. This was the name that went into his official records, like how our names are printed on our birth certificates. His friends called him Vishnu.

He was later known as Kautilya. Now, this name was unique to him. In history books and scholarly circles, the name Kautilya is quite well known."

I then realized why *Arthashastra* was linked to the name Kautilya, instead of Vishnugupta or Chanakya. But what exactly is *Arthashastra*? I was sure this question would be answered later. For now, I was still trying to understand the meaning of the name Kautilya.

"There are many stories and references about how he got the name Kautilya. There is a system in India called the *gotra* system. Names are given according to your *gotra* – your *Rishi* tradition. Scholars say, he was born under the *Kutila gotra*, and so, he was named Kautilya.

Another belief holds that his ancestors came from a village called Kutila. A school of thought in India, suggests that a person gets his name from his forefathers' place of origin. A person whose place of origin is Kutila, would, therefore, be called Kautilya.

Then grandpa presented a third, more convincing viewpoint:

"But the most famous belief holds that since he was a person who applied *Kuta Niti*, meaning shrewd tactics, to defeat his enemies, his name was kept as Kautilya.

The third name was most popular among the masses – Chanakya! This name comes from his father – Chanak. Chanak was a minister in the court of Dhanand, the last king of the Nanda Dynasty. As a scholar and an expert on political science, his son saw him as a role model. And so, Chanak's son was affectionately called Chanakya."

I understood later in my life that for every son, deep within, his father is a role model. The father-son relation is very unique.

For a child, his father is larger than life. But later, when the son becomes a father himself, he understands what a father goes through. From adoration to respect and reverence, a father and son are ever tuned to each other for life.

"Since the son adored his father, he also pursued the same profession – he went on to become a teacher of political science and a minister in the court of kings, advising and giving strategies for every situation.

Chanakya was a student and teacher at Takshashila university, one of the biggest universities of those times. He taught various methods on how to be a great king. Therefore, he was also known as a kingmaker."

Wow! I really liked the word 'kingmaker'.

"Who is more powerful: a king or a kingmaker?" Grandpa had opened a debate among us.

Most of us were of the same view and replied, "A king, of course."

What grandpa said next remained with me for life:

"You can become a king, but a king can lose his position over a period of time. A kingmaker, on the other hand, can make many kings. And the king will always be under the supervision, guidance and control of the kingmaker. So, he is very powerful. He rules without a position. He does not have power, yet he controls everything."

When I grew more responsible, I realized that kingmakers exist in the contemporary world as well. They exist in in every field: in politics, business, universities, government organizations, etc. It is better to be a kingmaker than be a king.

"Among the many students he trained was Chandragupta Maurya, the first king of the Maurya dynasty. Not that his other students did not become kings, but he was the shining example of Chanakya's principles. Among the examples of kings and kingmakers across the globe, India's Chanakya – Chandragupta combination is the one most often cited."

Chanakya's life is very exciting. It is full of stories and each event has an invaluable lesson to teach us. Grandpa, of course, could not narrate all the stories to us at one go; we heard them over various sessions, during which we had imbibed grandpa's lifelong efforts of reading books.

How Dhananand killed Chanak; how little Chanakya had to run away to save his life and complete his education; how he was the most-loved student at Takshashila Universityand then becoming a teacher himself. Finally, the return of Chanakya to defeat not just Dhananand, but Alexander as well.

I was extremely excited when grandpa mentioned Alexander. I had read about him in our school textbooks.

"Yes, the very same Alexander who wanted to conquer the world, but was defeated in India. The intelligence of one man – Chanakya – had sent back one of the greatest conquerors the world has ever known with his tail between his legs."

Each episode of Chanakya's life was worth exploring. He led a life of inspiration with his never-give-up attitude; not only was he a great teacher, but he was also a phenomenal strategist, thinker, scholar and a true patriot.

What a remarkable man!

Grandpa said, "While playing his multiple roles effectively, he always stood for *Dharma*."

"*Dharma*? What is that?" I asked.

"To understand the depth of this word, you need to study our ancient Indian scriptures. There is so much out there. But if you want to understand how to apply it in your day-to-day life, then study Kautilya's *Arthashastra*."

Finally, hereon began my introduction to the *Arthashastra* – the start of an everlasting pilgrimage to discovering the Chanakya in me.

# 4

# Artha-shastra?

Grandpa's copy of Kautilya's *Arthashastra* was thick, hardbound and its pages were written in Sanskrit. I had flipped through it and discovered many of the notes he had scribbled wherever space was available.

Apparently, grandpa also owned two translations of the *Arthashastra* – one in English and the other in his regional language. Perhaps comparing the translations allowed him to better understand the text, even though he was already a Sanskrit scholar and very well versed in English Literature.

When it came to understanding the *Arthashastra*, I could not understand even an iota of the huge book. The size of the book itself made me freeze in terror. Who would want to read such a book? Plus, it was in a strange, unfamiliar language called Sanskrit that almost seemed alien to me.

I had two questions in my mind: Why does the *Arthashastra* look so complicated? Is it necessary to learn Sanskrit to be able to understand Chanakya's teachings?

When I tossed these questions at grandpa, he gave me some profound answers:

"The *Arthashastra* is not simply a book, it is a philosophy, a *shastra,* or a scripture. *Shastras* are the wisdom of *Rishis* handed over from one generation to the next. If you want to understand these scriptures, you need a *Guru,* a teacher, who will unfold the wisdom within these scriptures in a way you can understand and appreciate them."

Addressing my query on Sanskrit, he said, "It is not necessary to know Sanskrit to study any shastra; however, knowing it gives you a very big advantage since most of our ancient scriptures are written in Sanskrit. You will also see that the language has a beauty of its own.

Even if you read scriptures translated into other languages, there will always be some limitation. Knowing the language in which the text was originally written will help you decode the scripture perfectly."

I knew how Indian culture glorified Sanskrit. "So, grandpa, is that the reason why Sanskrit is called the language of the Gods?"

Grandpa gave a mysterious smile, "The language of the Gods is Silence!

God cannot be understood through any language or logic. He is beyond both, yet language can take you there.

Through a good, scientific language like Sanskrit, you can understand the concept of God as experienced by our ancient saints and sages. Yet, being a scholar of Sanskrit alone does not help."

"Then what is it that helps us reach God?" This small boy had asked a deep question.

"Elimination of the ego." Grandpa's words put me into silence.

Looking deep into my eyes, he said, "Make sure that you learn Sanskrit language early on in your life."

My parents had me admitted to an English-medium school, so I had no academic orientation to the language at that point in life. But grandpa's advice, or rather instruction, remained in my heart forever. The seed that was sown was to take root and spring to life when the time was right.

In life, the right guidance at the right time makes all the difference. Chandragupta was just an ordinary boy before Chanakya made a king out of him. But creation of a king is not enough to run a kingdom; one has to know how to effectively lead a kingdom after becoming the king. This is the difference between an ordinary kingmaker and a kingmaker like Chanakya.

"People become kings or leaders through various methods: through money, power, hierarchy or various crooked means. Even if you do, you should atleast have the capability of leading your people after getting the position."

This was something I had never thought of. I had taken for granted that every prince would one day become a good king, but apparently, this was not the case.

"If the person is not capable, then he will not be able to keep his chair for long. That is why Chanakya wrote the *Arthashastra* – so that kings would know how to run their kingdom effectively after attaining of leadership."

Kautilya's *Arthashastra* was written like an instruction manual to help the king take decisions at every point of his life. It contains 6,000 sutras, which cover a wide range of subjects. It has over 180 topics covering theories of leadership, economics, appointment of ministers, eliminating criminals in society, maintenance of law and order, giving judgments and punishments, administration, foreign policy, warfare, international relations and many more."

My goodness! A king has to know all this? My hands and feet had already gone numb just listening to the long list grandpa had just spelt out. I do not want to ever become a king in my life. Who will learn all this?

I was never a top ranker in my school and never aimed to be one. And here was a book of instructions which insisted on the study of 6,000 sutras in Sanskrit – no way!

Grandpa must either be crazy or he must be a genius to first study the *Arthashastra* and then call it his favourite book. I wished to live a simple life. Why worry about the whole world, when you can lead a happy-go-lucky life?

Grandpa continued, "Apart from these topics, Chanakya was an expert on fort building, gemology, Ayurveda, weapons, medicines, psychology, philosophy and various other subjects.

No wonder people call him a rare master mind, who is remembered as the greatest strategist of all time."

This was all really exciting to learn. My admiration for Chanakya grew with each word grandpa spoke of him.

"Do you know Chanakya invented the game of chess?" grandpa asked.

"Chess?" Chanakya had just become all the more exciting.

"Chanakya taught everyone the right way of thinking. Chess was a game designed to train a person to think strategically."

Would any of you like to take a guess at what the word CHESS stands for?

# 5

# C-H-E-S-S

"Wars were very common in the olden days. Not that they do not take place in our times, but the number of battles fought was higher back then. To have a strong army and defeat the enemies was a major part of a king's job.

Chanakya had advised his students to be ever prepared for war. There is a very famous saying in the army: *Wars are not fought in the battlefield, but in the minds of the generals.*

Strategy was an important part of preparation in the army. Therefore, Chanakya placed great emphasis on strategic thinking. In the *Arthashastra,* it is called *Aanvikshiki.*"

*Aan-vik-shi-ki?* A tongue twister indeed! Trying to dig deeper, I asked, "What does *Aanvikshiki* mean, grandpa?"

"It is the science of strategic thinking based on philosophy."

Even as a child, I was absolutely spellbound by what I heard, but I did not understand a thing beyond that. I did not want to get into some philosophical discussion at that point either; I just wanted to hear more of the story. Trying to change the topic, I asked, "Grandpa, what is the connection between chess and Chanakya?"

"If you look at the game of chess, it is a war game. It consists of strategic moves one makes against one's enemy. Something like a simulation game."

He then took us through the fundamentals of the game: "There are two parties with equal power – the same number of soldiers, elephants, horses, etc. But the winner is the one who pulls the best strategic moves."

That day, I understood one thing about power: it was not about what or who you had on your side, but how you used them that mattered.

"Chanakya wanted his students to think strategically in any given situation; that is what makes a person a winner or a loser," grandpa said.

To make us put on our thinking caps, he asked, "What do you think is the best way to developing strategic thinking?"

It seemed like an odd question to ask. We all looked at each other, as if asking, "Can strategic thinking really be developed?" Well, this was news to all of us!

In a deliberately low voice grandpa said, "The best way to develop strategic thinking is to... play games!"

Which child would not be delighted on hearing such an answer? Parents stopped us from playing too much and made studies and homework our first priority. Meanwhile, our grandpa here was suggesting the complete opposite!

"But don't play games for the sake of playing. *Think* while you play a game. In any game there will be winners and losers, but both can be learners. The one who keeps learning, keeps improving and winning becomes natural for him."

Bringing the *Arthashastra* back into the discussion, he said, "Out of 15 books of the *Arthashastra*, 8 deal with the preparation for a war and fighting it. The more you plan during peacetime, the less you bleed during wartime. Planning is more important than execution; in fact, better planning helps in effective execution.

In those days, there was a particular formation of the army, similar to the game of chess. It was called *Chaturanga*. *Chatur* is four and *anga* is parts. Therefore, it means four parts of an army."

Taking us through the ancient ways of fighting wars, he explained: "The men of an army went to war in four ways – on foot, called infantry; riding horses; driven in chariots; and mounted on elephants.

Each person in the formation showed his power and rank, based on the mode of transport he employed while marching onto the battlefield.

Chanakya, therefore, wanted his students to prepare for war before it was to actually happen. You see, this was how the world's first war game, *Chaturanga*, was born. Two friends could sit and play the game even within the comforts of a palace. It helped them come up with innovative methods for fighting a war."

Nice idea, I thought. Practice fighting before the actual fight. It made sense to me.

Another curious cousin of mine asked grandpa, "But, grandpa, in the game of chess there are camels too."

"That is a good observation." Grandpa always encouraged independent thinking. "Over time, the game of *Chaturanga* went through many changes. Even in war, there were alterations, such as the use of other animals, like the camels in desert areas. Camels are employed by our army even today in states like Rajasthan and Gujarat, as these animals know the region well and so, are very useful.

As the game became popular, traders who came to India took it to other countries. When they played the game in the

Arab world, camels became an essential element of war; that is why we find camels included in chess today. When it went to European nations, more modifications were made to the game. To this day, however, the fundamentals of chess lie in the *Arthashastra*."

Then came the real eye-opener for all of us:

"Do you know that chess is actually an abbreviation, a short form of a number of words? Can you guess what the full form is?

C - Chariots

H - Horses

E - Elephants

S - Soldier(s)

And so, *Chaturanga* became C-H-E-S-(S)."

Now that we were able to relate the past to the present, our chests swelled with pride thinking about our country.

"But grandpa, I do not want to be a king; I'm not interested at all," I interrupted, letting him know that all this talk was fine, but not useful to me.

"Who said Chanakya's ideas are only meant for those who want to be kings?" he shot back. "It does not matter who you are or what area of work you are in. Kautilya's *Arthashastra* is useful to everyone."

"Everyone?" My eyes widened in surprise.

"Yes, everyone who wants to be a leader, no matter what kind of work they do."

That made sense to me. I wanted to be a leader, but how… ?

# 6

# Bringing Out the Leader in Me

"Leadership is a very interesting concept," grandpa said. "It has various dimensions. It is the ability to lead people to a higher goal; the clarity to take decisions in difficult circumstances; making the impossible possible; inspiring a group and walking the talk. It is not just about knowing the rules of the game, but winning the game. Above all, it is the ability to see things where others do not."

These were the first thoughts on leadership that were etched in my mind and heart. "How does one become a leader?" I asked eagerly.

"Good question," grandpa was inspired by my enthusiasm. "There are many methods to becoming a leader – by reading books on leadership, associating with other leaders, learning from the lives of other leaders and thinking about leaders. In short, to become a leader, one should be able to think and act like a leader."

The wise man continued, "Leadership is not just about a position or power of authority that you hold; it is also being morally right."

"Morally right? What does that mean?"

"According to our Indian scriptures, a leader has to be *Dharmic* first. He has to be righteous. That is the reason the ideal king is known as *Raja-Rishi* – a sage-like king or a philosopher king."

"Why does one need to be *Dharmic* to be a leader?" I wanted to know.

"The greatest dilemma a leader faces is called *Dharma Sankat*. This involves deciding what is right and what is wrong, and then taking actions based on the decision."

As if the leader in me had been awakened, I asked, "So by studying the *Arthashastra*, does one become a leader?"

"The *Arthashastra* was written only for leaders, and only leaders can understand its content completely; the rest will miss the point."

Taking the topic to different plane altogether, grandpa then said, "But before one studies the *Arthashastra,* one should study the *Bhagavad Gita* first."

*Bhagavad Gita?* How were the two books even related?

"As I just mentioned, *Dharma Sankat* or moral dilemma is the greatest challenge that a leader faces. The *Bhagavad Gita* addresses the *Dharma Sankat* of Arjun, the greatest warrior-leader, as he is in the midst of battle.

Arjun was more than capable of fighting the war, but when it came to taking action on the battlefield, he developed cold feet. He was suffering from confusion of the highest degree – should he fight his relatives or not?"

The solution?

"Then comes Krishna, who gives him spiritual and material advice. This dialogue between Krishna and Arjun makes up the *Bhagavad Gita*. Krishna's guidance ultimately helped lift Arjun's morale to win the war. Krishna advises Arjun not only on *Dharma Sankat,* but also on the various strategies and tactics required in different situations during the *Mahabharata* war."

I remembered the many stories grandpa had narrated to us about the war during our previous trip.

"So, with the *Bhagavad Gita* as a base, when you study the *Arthashastra,* a king becomes an ideal king. He becomes a *Dharmic* king not just in theory, but also in practice, combining his knowledge of philosophy and strategy. Both the books have the objective of bringing out the decision-maker in you; to bring out the leader in you."

Did grandpa bring out the leader in me at that point?

"To bring out the leader in you, you should be able to bring out the Chanakya in you. The *Arthashastra* will help you in this regard."

Little did I know that from that point onwards, both the *Bhagavad Gita* and *Arthashastra* would be my guiding forces in life forever.

Grandpa also warned me, "Remember, do not look at leadership only from a king's point of view. In today's democratic world, every person can be a king. The *Arthashastra* can be used by both men and women, by people in various fields and professions, by people across nations and generations."

This was an introduction to a new dimension for me. Even though Chanakya had advised Chandragupta and Krishna had advised Arjun, the same message was meant for you and me, for everyone. It was universal. Anyone could pick up these gems of knowledge and use them in their lives.

As a child, I did not know what profession I would choose for myself, but I decided that regardless of my choice, I would surely aim to be a leader, an inspiration and a positive contributor.

Our short vacation had come to an end. Every holiday ended with very painful parting moments full of tears. Still, as always, we looked forward to the next vacation. During the journey back to the city, I pondered over all the wisdom my grandpa had given us.

In those quiet moments sitting alone, I took some decisions that would have an impact on my life forever. Little did I know that this was the last time I would see grandpa.

Within a few days, grandpa passed away. It happened so suddenly and my parents felt that it was not important for me to rush to our native place for the funeral the way they had to. It was the 13th day of the ceremony when I finally arrived and all our relatives had gathered together.

I wished I could see grandpa at least one more time. I looked for him all around the house, but I knew he was gone... gone forever.

In my search for him, I went to his library. I walked up to the chair, where he had sat and told us many enthralling stories, one after another.

Then I noticed his favourite book – Kautilya's *Arthashastra* lying on the table. The book was open; it seemed as though he had been reading it even on the last day of his life. Who would've thought that from that moment on, his favourite book would become my favourite book.

I could not resist picking it up. I took it to grandma and asked her, "Grandma, can I take this book with me?"

She said, "Take it. He left all the books for you."

# 7

# A Love for Books

Death gives a new perspective to life.

Grandpa's was the first death that I had experienced in my life. I did cry for a few days, because I missed him terribly. However, my parents told me that sooner or later, death will come to all of us.

The question was not whether a person lived a long life, but whether he led a life of inspiration. Some people live as if they are already dead, while others live on even after their physical death.

A very interesting take on the subject lies within the pages of another book that I read later in my life – *Kathopanishad*. It is a very different book.

In this *Upanishad*, a young boy named Nachiketa has a dialogue with Yama, the lord of death. Nachiketa questions the very existence and permanency of a person on this planet Earth and what happens after death.

I knew grandpa was physically gone, but for all of us, he had left a treasure chest of evergreen memories. He also had given us valuable tips on how to lead a quality life.

Life moved on and I grew up in the hustle and bustle of a

busy city. Yet, I held onto the best gift grandpa had left me – my love for books. I had picked up majority of the books from his library, when my father said, "We do not have enough space at home." Some of the books I had picked up included the *Vedas*, the *Bhramasutras*, the *Mahabharata* and the life of saints. Not that I read all the books, but somewhere, preserved in their pages, my grandpa was still speaking to me.

I was not a class topper, but neither was I among the last benchers. I was an average student. Never did I fail in school or college, but neither did I aim to be number one in class. But yes, there was something about me that even the class toppers, teachers and friends appreciated – my love for books.

Whenever I had free time during school or college hours, I used to go to the library. Not that I did not enjoy time out with my friends, go for movies or have street food on the limited budget that a student usually keeps.

In between all that, I used to sneak into the library and peep into every possible book. In fact, among my friends, it became a well-known fact and ultimately a time-tested solution; if I was not around, their conclusion was: "We will find him in the library."

The college librarian loved me. I was among the few students who would read all types of books, not just text books. From science fictions to novels, ancient Indian literature to modern management – I tried to get a feel of everything.

The librarian used to even give me some tips: "Here is a new book. Try it, you will love it." He was like an ice cream vendor; whenever a new flavour would come into the market, he wanted me to taste it.

I loved the smell of books. I never felt alone among them. I felt like I belonged there with them; I felt at home among them. A book can be your best friend. This friend has a viewpoint to offer, yet does not object to your opinion. I did not just read books; I loved to listen to them. Books speak to those who want to listen.

The library used to conduct book discussions, and I used to attend all of them. They were very healthy and intellectual interactions. Even my scholarly, more studious friends loved me, because every time they had a discussion, I was able to contribute. I almost felt like I was an intellectual too!

One day, a notice regarding a book launch was put up in the college library. The venue was at the other end of the city. The author was going to be accompanied by a celebrity at the launch. I really wanted to know what happens at a book launch, but since none of my friends were interested, I decided to go alone.

It was an experience of a lifetime. The bookstore was huge and its numerous shelves were brimming with books. The surroundings may have been simple, but with so many people gathered for the event, there was something glamorous about it too.

The celebrity was a film director, who was a book lover himself. And for this reason, he had agreed to release the book of a comparatively unknown author. I guess most of the crowd came to the event to see the famous director, rather than to read the book or meet the author.

But, the celebrity made a noteworthy comment: "Friends, today we are surrounded by lakhs of books. These are not just books, but the experiences of lakhs of people, each of whom have experienced life differently from us."

Someone asked the author about what inspired him to write a book. He said, "Reading makes you a man, while writing makes you a complete man." He wrote the book to find a sense of fulfillment within himself.

I reflected on my own life; I had collected books throughout my life, despite space and money constraints. My mother said, "Why don't you join a circulating library? So that after reading it, you can return the book." This was a space-saving idea, but who can replace the joy of owning a book, of scribbling notes on the pages and referring to it at any point in life? Who knew that this love for books would make me a bestselling author in the years to come!

Collecting and reading books is one thing, but gathering useful notes from them is another.

Let me explain...

# 8

# Notes on Chanakya

A teacher once told me, "To understand a subject, one needs to do three types of reading; rather, read it three times, but from different angles." She continued, "The first time you read a book for a research paper, it should be general reading, almost like taking a glance. Check if the subject is of interest to you or not. If there is no connect, just drop the book." This was a good time-management tip, since in today's world, millions of books are being published across the globe.

"If the book interests you, do a second round of reading. This time, it is serious work. Take a pen or pencil and make notes. If there are questions, get clarity on them and seek answers from experts." No wonder, this teacher was highly respected for her contribution to the field of education.

"The third type of reading is called revision reading. After clearing all your doubts, you revisit the book. This time, you are almost like an expert on the subject." She further added, "Now, you can also go and give a presentation on the book to others." I loved this idea – from being a reader of a book, you become a speaker on the book!

An idea, a possibility started to take shape in my mind.

The interest in Chanakya's life had been there since childhood. Thanks grandpa!

Over a period of time, I had collected many books on Chanakya. Some of them were from street vendors, some from big bookshops and some while traveling through various towns and cities. I was quite surprised that a large number of people had written on Chanakya over many generations.

Books on his life and his teachings were also available in many different languages. Some books were scholarly and academic in nature, while others were for general reading. Some of them made sense, while others repeated stories that had already been told, but presented in a different format. But now I wanted to go beyond the story of Chanakya.

The most popular book on Chanakya was *Chanakya Niti*, which gave advice to a common man on how to lead a good and prosperous life. It was simple enough to understand. Other books on Chanakya's thoughts included *Niti Shastra* and *Chanakya Praniti Sutra*. The book called *Mudrarakshasa* was a drama based on Chanakya's life and his strategy to dethrone the king Dhanananda. And then, of course, was my grandpa's favourite – Kautilya's *Arthashastra*.

I made notes from all the books and maintained them in a file, storing them away for future reference. From time to time, I quoted a few stories to impress my friends and teachers. But again, the *Arthashastra* stood apart from all the other books. It was deep and profound, but it was not easy to understand in the first reading. I had to concentrate really hard in order to understand it. Some notes that grandpa had made in his copy were very useful to me.

I guess I had understood some bits and pieces of Chanakya's life, yet I felt that I had not understood it all. Was my madam wrong when she said that three readings would make one an expert?

I had read the entire *Arthashastra* over ten times now. It contained 6,000 sutras and I had read every one of them with all my sincerity, but I still felt like I had missed something.

One day, my father took me to a *satsangh*, a spiritual discourse. Attending spiritual discourses was a part of our family culture. That day, the *Sadhu* who was giving the spiritual discourse said something interesting:

"To understand a scripture, you require four types of *Krupa*, or grace: *Atma Krupa, Ishwar Krupa, Guru Krupa* and *Shastra Krupa*.

*Atma Krupa* is the grace you give yourself through self efforts. No lazy person can ever understand any scripture. You need sincerity and dedication in your study of the scriptures." Well, I guess I had made all the necessary efforts.

"*Ishwar Krupa* is the grace of god on you. If you take one step towards god, god will take ten steps towards you. The more efforts you put in, the more likely it is that the grace of god will be awakened." I wondered if despite all my efforts, there was a lack of god's grace on me.

"*Guru Krupa* is the grace of your teacher. Never study the *Shastras* alone. It should be done under the guidance of an expert teacher. The teacher will open up unknown dimensions about the scripture to you." This raised another question in my mind: does one really require a teacher to study a scripture?

"Lastly, *Shastra Krupa* is the grace of the scripture itself. The scripture that you study should open up to you. There are many people who study various scriptures, yet you will find them hollow. They speak about the scripture, but it is the scripture that has to speak to you." Well, here was something that I never knew.

That night, I started to reflect on my own method of studying Chanakya and his teachings. Right from the interest grandpa had created in my childhood towards his stories to reading books, making notes and devoting my efforts, I had probably done everything I could. Yet, the four *krupas* were not complete... I still required more types of grace: God's grace, *Guru*'s grace and the grace of scriptures.

The next morning, I went back to the *Sadhu*, whom we referred to as *Swamiji*. "*Swamiji*, how does one attain all the graces you mentioned? I want to understand the *Arthashastra* and Chanakya completely. He is a mystery to me and to our generation. Is it possible to understand Chanakya in totality?"

"Nothing is impossible according to Indian tradition, but to understand the scriptures, follow the time-tested *Guru-Shishya* and *Gurukul* method of studies."

"What are these methods?"

He started to deliver another *satsangh*...

# 9

# *Guru* – The Greatest

The *Sadhu* was a man of wisdom. He was much like my grandfather, who had a way of describing profound concepts in a simple manner. Or was it that I was searching for my grandpa in every wise person I met, and in every good storyteller I came across?

As I matured, I understood that certain people do not die at all. Yes, at the physical level, one may turn back into dust, but the ideas and ideals that one believed in, live on forever.

Mature… my mind lingered on the word briefly, while taking me back to the time when grandpa had told me its meaning.

"Grandpa, when I grow up, will I become mature?"

"It is when you are mature that you grow up."

Yes, I had grown up, but there was still a long way to go as far as becoming mature was concerned.

"There are two things that you must learn in order to understand the culture and tradition of India," said the *Sadhu*, drawing my attention back to the present.

"First, the *Guru-Shishya Parampara.*" It was as though he was transported to a different world while explaining it, "The *Guru* is not just a teacher like the kind we have in schools and colleges today. The *Guru* does not just take a class to teach a particular subject. He is not just a professionally-qualified individual who gives lectures. A *Guru* teaches a subject, no doubt, but he has a higher responsibility to guide the student from the concerned subject to godhood.

A *Guru* may teach a formal subject, such as science, mathematics, accounts or languages, but through the subject, he will slowly take you towards understanding the meaning of life.

It is not when his student becomes a first ranker that the *Guru* becomes happy, but when he becomes a good human being. Therefore, a *Guru* is a wise person who wants you to become wise, too – both in the worldly and spiritual sense.

And a *Shishya,* or a student, too, is not an ideal student if he or she stands first in class or makes lots of money in his career. The student should be attuned to the *Guru*, both in mind and thought, forever."

I wondered if such concepts still existed in our modern education system.

"The *Guru-Shishya* relationship is a divine one. There is a lot of *Shraddha* or faith in each other. A *Guru* imparts his knowledge in its entirety and a *Shishya* gathers the same through his dedicated *Seva* or service to the *Guru*."

For a moment, I became silent and asked myself, do I have a *Guru* in life or have I just had subject teachers all around me?

As if reading my mind, the *Sadhu* said, "The real *Guru* is god and no one else. God comes to us in the form of a *Guru*, but for that to happen, you need to be an ideal *Shishya,* who is ready for knowledge.

In India, even today we consider our *Guru* as the greatest – even above our parents, who are our first *Gurus* and teachers. Even the most powerful kings and monarchs used to bow down to their *Gurus.*

Second is the *Gurukul* model of teaching. The ashram or hermitage where the *Guru* stays is called the *Gurukul*. Students from all over the world would go and stay there with him to study."

"Like a modern-day hostel in colleges?" I tried to clarify.

"Not really. There is a major difference," he said. "In a modern-day system, a hostel is more like accommodation provided to the students. The only connect between the teacher and student is during the classroom sessions. During the remaining part of the day, the teacher and students are in their own worlds." He had a point!

"While in a *Gurukul*, the *Guru* and the students lived like a family. They cared for each other, helped each other in daily chores and even knew each other very personally. The students learnt not just through the lessons in class, but also from their *Guru*'s behaviour."

He then made a powerful point: "A student learned from his *Guru* in three ways – through his *Aachaar* (his conduct), *Vichaar* (his thoughts and ideas) and *Vyavahaar* (his interaction and behaviour with others); all three were linked to each other.

The *Guru* was a role model. In the *Gurukul* system, learning took place 24/7. They learnt by just being around their *Guru* and observing him closely. They learnt during their formal and informal interactions with him, as well as through the daily classes he took."

I left Swamiji's place later that day, having understood the basis of the Indian tradition of keeping knowledge alive through the *Guru-Shishya* and *Gurukul* methods. I realized that I had read the *Arthashastra* many times over and that meant that I probably had the *Atma Krupa* of self-effort. But the remaining three – *Ishwar Krupa, Guru Krupa* and *Shastra Krupa* – were missing.

Where could I find a *Guru* who would teach me the *Arthashastra* through the ancient methods? Was I an ideal *shishya?* Did *Gurukuls* exist even today, which were more like a family than a hostel? Where was I to go to seek these answers?

My grandparents were gone, but my parents were still around. Over time, my father and mother had become my role models.

I rushed home and as I entered, said, "Papa, I need a little help…"

# 10

# From Grandpa to Papa

I was born into a family that was quite progressive in its thinking. Since childhood, I had seen different kinds of people from all walks of life visit our home.

Long hours of discussion were a common scene in our house. Right from politics to the latest trends in science, from music and arts to business trends, one could hear a host of topics being discussed.

Both my parents were well read and well versed in global affairs, but what stood out was the spiritual culture that ran like an undercurrent in our house.

I am not saying that we were a religious family, but we were a spiritual family in the true sense.

Of course, we celebrated all the Indian festivals and had daily rituals and regular poojas at home. Yet, we also had various spiritual masters come to our house and discuss philosophy. These masters were either individuals or from various spiritual organizations, and there were even followers of different religions. Discussions went beyond the *Mahabharata* and *Ramayana* to *The Bible, Quran, Guru Granth Sahib* and *Agamas*. It was an open culture, ready to explore new philosophical dimensions.

Grandpa used to say, "Arguments are different from discussions. In arguments, one wants to prove that he is right; while in discussions, one wants to know *what* is right."

We discussed and debated to find the truth. At times, we never accepted the other person's point of view, yet we respected him as an individual. Like me, grandpa had also influenced my papa a lot. It was later that I came to know that my papa had maintained notes about what his father had discussed with him.

In fact, we had one of grandpa's sayings framed on the wall in our house. Papa said, "I do not know the source of this saying, but for me, since I heard it from my father, I give the credit to him."

The framed saying was: *I may not agree with what you say, but till my death, I will not take away your freedom to disagree with me.*

Whenever any argument escalated into a big fight, one of us would point to the framed quote and suddenly, smiles would appear on our faces.

My mother, too, was a very pious lady with a brilliant intellect. At times, she surprised all of us with her viewpoint. She used to make us think in a new direction. If my father could quote Bhishma's advice from the *Mahabharata*, my mother could offer a counter quote from the *Jataka Tales*.

Life at home was full of fun and learning. As they say, I must have done some punya in my previous birth to be born into such a great family. I was indeed blessed.

"Papa, I want to study Kautilya's *Arthashastra* in the traditional *Guru-Shisya* and *Gurukul* method." Though this seemed more like an announcement, what I really wanted was an opinion and not just from papa, but both my parents.

Even before he could think, mummy was ready with her reply. I guess it's a common scene in every house, where women are ready to share their views, sometimes even it has not been asked for!

"So, finally the time has come. I knew it the very day you went to meet grandpa all alone in his room, when we all went to the village market." Well, who says women do not understand human psychology?

"Scriptures have a way of attracting you," Papa added. "Once the call comes, no one can resist. In our tradition, it is referred to as the 'Call of the *Rishis*'. When the call comes, no power on earth can stop you."

My goodness! This was the most profound statement I had ever heard from my father in all these years. He was speaking exactly like my grandpa. Of course, he was the son of the same man, so he had it in his DNA. Modern science has proved that finally, it is all about genetics. The wisdom had been transferred from grandpa to papa. And now it was probably time to transfer it to me.

There is an age-old saying: *Your mother takes you to your father, and your father takes you to your Guru.*

When a child is born, it is only the mother the child associates with. Then, slowly the mother introduces the child to his father. And when the time of education comes, the father puts him under the guidance of a *Guru*.

"There is a system in our tradition called *Vidya-Arambham* – the beginning of one's education. Some people also call it *Upanayanam,* or putting on the sacred thread. It is also called initiation into the great Vedic knowledge," Papa explained.

"Be it a king's son, or a farmer's son or that of a trader or labourer, all were entitled to equal education. After the *Vidya-Arambham* ceremony, the parents handed over the child to the *Guru*. Then, the child would spend the next phase of his life in the *Gurukul* for many years."

"How many years?" I asked.

"The average was 12 to 14 years, but the decision was taken by the *Guru*, depending on the student's capability and capacity. After his education, the child was sent back to the city to live a productive life among his family and society."

"Where is my *Gurukul*, papa?" He smiled as if he had prepared the answer many years ago...

# 11

# One Teacher, One Student

It was a unique stage in my life, or should I call it a major turning point in my life. My college exams were just two months away. This was my final year in college. I would then be called a graduate!

In India, becoming a graduate is typically a big thing, or some say, a normal thing. It is as if your formal education is over and you now have to look out for a job and start earning.

In my college, some students were already working part-time and getting some income. Some needed the extra money to support their parents, who were not that well to do. Some, in spite of being well off, joined other companies or their own family businesses. This is because, at the end of the day, everyone felt that the end of education should ideally be the beginning of a working life.

Our society has a strange problem. Every person we meet will ask us the standard question: "What do you do?" In short, it means, "what do you do for a living?" The answer expected is an economic activity: "I work in this company", "I am a doctor", "I am a businessman".

In my later years, I learnt that in different cultures like in Europe, the answers to this question are more along the lines of "I play football", "I am a painter", "I write books".

For them, the question meant, what is your passion? What is your hobby? What do you really love to do in life? Your profession is built around your passion. While in India, it is your profession first and then the rest of all that you love – either a hobby or a weekend activity, that follows.

The reason for this situation is due to various factors. We are a growing economy, after having regained our freedom from foreign rule. Back then, a person had to take care of not only himself, but also his family – and a family was usually large in size; one could not think only about his individual self in India.

Apart from a person's own wife and kids, he had to think of his parents, grandparents and many other relatives and friends. He had to take up responsibilities, like educating himself and his siblings, getting his sister married, taking care of aging parents and also contributing to other social activities.

"What do you do?" When someone asked me this question, one answer came quite spontaneously: "I am studying in college." That was enough for the other person to keep quiet. Most of them would not even try to probe any further.

But in two months' time, I needed to have a different answer. Either I had to take up a new course, so that the standard answer continued – "I am doing my masters" – or I had to take up some economic activity. Otherwise, I would become a social misfit. People would begin to consider me useless and unproductive.

But, what papa said at that critical moment in my life, was very out-of-the-box thinking.

"Once the college exams are over, take a break. Go and stay in a *Gurukul*. Do not worry about your future, but go and create your own future. Spend time with yourself. Explore within. Reflect about life. And in the *Gurukul,* study the *Arthashastra* under the guidance of a *Guru.*"

How lucky I was to have a father like him, who did not want me to become another stereotype!

Mummy added, "Son, in a *Gurukul,* you will be exposed to a strange environment that is meditative and contemplative. There is a divine presence in such places. You will feel secure and safe."

Most mothers are worried about their children and their safety. And here was mine, who along with my father, was asking me to head to a *Gurukul* to find a sense of direction to take my life forward.

Papa said, "There are various forms of *Gurukuls*. It could be an institution with over thousands of students. It could be an ashram with spiritual seekers. It could be a research place, or it could be "one teacher-one student" type, too. Which type of *Gurukul* would you like to go to?"

The question took me by surprise. I did not know that there were so many options available to me! To begin with, I was lucky enough to explore life itself; now, I could explore different types of *Gurukuls*. But it seemed difficult for me to pick from the choices available.

First of all, I was being introduced to the *Gurukul* system for the first time, so which one am I to choose? Secondly, how do I know the difference between the types unless I go through the processes myself? It was like going to a new place and then someone asks you what your favourite local dish is.

Truly speaking, you do not have an option but to ask the other person, a local himself, to give his suggestions on the matter. There is one other option – ask for a buffet. Taste a bit of everything, so you do not feel you missed out on anything.

Reflecting on the food varieties, I told papa, "I would like to go to a *Gurukul* which gives me a taste of all the formats of *Gurukuls* available." I wanted academic research as a base; I wanted the spiritual ambience; I wanted other friends around me too. Yet, the most appealing was...

The "one teacher-one student" relationship.

Papa picked up his diary and showed me a telephone number, saying, "Call this person. You will find your *Arthashastra Guru.*"

# 12

# The Six-Month Farewell

He was a Sanskrit scholar and had been a university professor for over 35 years. Since he was to retire soon, he had a greater urge to spread his knowledge. Usually, when a person retires, people believe that his career has ended. Few understand that it is the opening of a new chapter in life; it is the second innings of the game.

The difference this time is that you play the game in a better manner. The first part of your life goes into making money, taking care of your family, educating your children and addressing other responsibilities that life brings you. In the second innings, when you retire, your children have all been settled and your finances are well taken care of. Most of your worldly responsibilities have been fulfilled.

Now, if you still have a healthy body and a fit mind, you have two choices: either you pull on, waiting for a comfortable death, or you take up a new passion and vision in life.

For many people who have a vision beyond a mundane life, retirement is only a blessing. It gives you the freedom to do what you want. You not only have the freedom, but also the maturity to take the next step.

"Sir, I would like to study the *Arthasastra*," I said, when he answered the call.

"It's not *Arthasastra*. It is *Arthashastra*." He emphasized, "It is 'sha' not 'sa'."

I had already made my first mistake before I could even be considered as a student by this great well-known Sanskrit scholar. Imagine my position at that moment! I had read the book *Arthashastra* over and over again, and also silently considered myself an expert. And now that I was speaking on the phone for the first time with the man I hoped would become my *Guru*, I go and make a mistake on the keyword itself!

Clean bowled in the very first ball!

"Sir, my father said you are the right person to teach me the *Arthashastra*. Will you become my *Guru*?" I was struggling to make sure that I conveyed carefully why I had called him. I guess such requests for him were very common, so he did not seem excited about what I wanted from him. I am sure as a university professor, he would have had no trouble attracting students.

"Why do you want to study the *Arthashastra*?" He was trying to understand the objective of my interest.

I did not know how to reply. "Just like that," I managed.

"Just like that?" he asked in surprise. I knew that people would not study any ancient Indian book just like that, especially in the career-obsessed world that I was exposed to, so this did not seem like a logical answer.

"Do you want to get into academics and take up the *Arthashastra* as some research project?"

I realized that most of the students who must have approached him at the university would have asked for his guidance to get into another academic job as a career. At times, such specialized research on a book like the *Arthashastra* would add value to your curriculum vitae and get you a government college job as a Sanskrit teacher.

"What is your qualification in Sanskrit?"

I froze when he asked me this question. I had never studied Sanskrit in my life. I had no basic qualification at all and here I was, talking to a man considered to be a living god of the language.

"No basic qualification?" His tone indicated that I had shocked him a second time. I had already lost hope and thought of hanging up the call. Mentally, I was prepared to forget the *Arthasastra*, sorry *Arthashastra,* for life.

"What has inspired you to study the *Arthashastra* then?"

Now this was the only question that I could answer confidently and truthfully, "My grandfather was a scholar of the *Arthashastra*. He had introduced me to the book as a child, but I never got the chance to study the same under a *Guru*."

There was a silence at the other end for a few moments. He seemed to be thinking.

"Have you read the *Arthashastra* before?"

Now, here I was full of confidence. As if a dead man had come back to life, I said in a louder voice, "Yes sir, many times. I have read all the 6000 sutras, but only in English. I tried reading them in Sanskrit, but could not grasp all the details of the language."

"Okay, that is good. So, you do have some background." Well, it seemed as though I had passed the test – almost. "Can you come here for six months?"

Yes, I had been accepted!

"Yes, sir, whatever you say." I wanted to surrender to my newfound *Guru*.

He was due to complete his last assignment at the university in the next few months and I had a couple of months to go before I completed my graduation; it was just perfect. Over the next few phone calls, we took some decisions. I had to go to the village he stayed in. There was an ashram there that had a research library in it.

This ashram was close to his house. He would only take about two hours of class per day. The remaining part of the day would be spent studying in the ashram's library. The ashram was also where I would be staying in the village.

I was so excited about going from the city to the village, that over the next few months, taking my final exams became only a formality. I was eagerly waiting for the new chapter of my life to begin.

And then, the day arrived...

# 13

# The Journey Within

There is a saying: *Fear is always about the unknown*. Here I was, standing in front of the mirror, looking at myself. I did not know what the future had in store for me; it was unknown. Yet, I was very happy inside. It was all so exciting.

The person in the mirror told me, "You are going on a journey not outside, but within yourself. It is a journey from the unknown to the known. It is not just about learning the *Arthashastra;* it is about how to live the *Arthashastra*."

And the same voice said, almost more deliberately: "You are not just going to discover the wisdom of Chanakya; you are going to discover the... *Chanakya in You*."

I woke up from the dream when my mother called out to me: "Come on, it's time to leave! Hope you have kept the food packet in your bag. Don't forget that!"

This was the first time in my life that I was going away from home for so long. I had gone out with my friends on picnics and outings for a few days at a time, but this was the first time that I was going alone, and that too, for six months straight.

My friends could not understand what I was trying to do

with my life; they thought I was going to some random village to study some strange Sanskrit book. As if they were sure of what they were going to do with their own lives! Hah!

I did try to explain to them, "I am going to study Kautilya's *Arthashastra* under the guidance of a *Guru* through the *Guru-Shishya* tradition by staying in an ashram."

Even though they did not say anything to my face, I was sure that it must have started a chain of gossip that I had gone crazy. I had overheard a friend of mine saying: "Sanskrit and godly ideas are meant to be studied after retirement. We are in the prime of youth; we must focus on building our careers first." I decided not to react at that point and instead, left all the questions to be answered by time itself.

As I boarded the train, my mother had tears in her eyes. However, I knew that they were not tears of sadness or separation, but tears of joy. She was happy that her son was taking a path few dared to take – to study our ancient Indian literature.

I know that when a mother parts from her children, she is concerned about their safety and security. But, being deeply spiritual, my mother always believed that in the journey of life, god is your ultimate protector and provider.

Father wore a detached look. He had made sure that I knew the directions, had given me enough money to take care of myself and had also given a personal call to my newfound *Guru* to ensure that his boy was guided properly.

I touched my parents' feet and took their blessings. Mentally, I also took the blessings of my grandparents. My grandpa's words had become a part of my thoughts.

I also recollected the words of the *Sadhu*, who had touched my life through various *satsanghs*: "Saints never fail to have an impact on a person's life. Their teachings are like seeds that lay hidden in the soil; when the time comes, they take root and grow into a huge tree."

How many saints had blessed my life since childhood? My grandparents, my parents, the *Sadhu* who guided me and this new *Guru* I was about to meet. I guess life was full of *satsanghs* – the company of people with noble thoughts.

As the train started out, I felt blessed. It was a two-day journey. I spent my time reading and revising the *Arthashastra*, using my grandfather's original copy. Somewhere deep within, I was also preparing for another test.

I was going to meet my *Arthashastra Guru* for the first time and I was afraid he might ask me a question from the book, so I should have my answers ready.

I did not want to repeat the mistake I had made during the informal telephonic interview he had taken the first time. "*Arthashastra*, not *Arthasastra*." I would make sure this time that 'sh' was pronounced clearly. I guess I had never ever prepared for any exam in school or college the way I was preparing to meet this *Guru* of mine. Had I done so, I am sure I would have topped every class.

The train arrived at its destination. It was afternoon when I alighted onto the platform of this small station. I dragged my luggage to the bus stop in the hot sun. The bus ride was another one-hour journey to my *Guru's* house.

The long journey had drained me of energy. I was hungry too, but just after sipping some water, I moved forward with full curiosity to meet the man who would change my destiny forever. As I got down from the bus, a small shopkeeper guided me to my *Guru's* house. This village had large houses compared to those in the city. As I passed by many of them, everyone looked at me curiously. I felt like an alien creature, who had just landed on planet Earth. And then in front of me was the gate; I opened it. It made a sound similar to a door bell. I could make out some movement within the house. Two people emerged and walked towards me.

The first one was surely my *Guru*.

But who was the other person... ?

# 14

# My *Arthashastra Guru*

"Your father had called. He wanted to know if you had arrived." My *Guru* was not as curious about me as I was about him; at least, it seemed so. He took me into his house.

I guess many students like myself had come to his house for some tips on Sanskrit. For me, he was my *Guru*, but *Guruji* had many *shishyas*. What else could you expect from a man who had spent 35 years teaching at a university?

He was slim and fit. He had grey hair, which I think is the minimum requirement to be a *Guru*. If you have no evidence of age *on* your head, people will think you do not have anything *inside* your head.

The other person who was with him was his wife. My father had given me enough details about my *Guru's* family before I had started from home. His wife said, "Hope you did not have any difficulty in finding this place.

It's a little towards the innermost sections of the village, so you need to walk from the bus stop, but you will never get lost here. Every village is safe, unlike a city."

*Guruji* had already started sharing some of his wisdom as I was entering his large house: "Do you know the difference between a village and a city?" He wanted to test me again, I thought.

Before I could say anything, he answered the question himself, "In a village, the first person knows the last person and in a city, the first person does not even know the next person." It was deeper than what it seemed.

He explained further: "A village is not just a place of habitation; it's a larger family. Everyone knows each other well. They are part of each other's joys and sorrows. If there is a problem faced by one person, the entire village comes to help him." Yes, I remembered how the whole village used to flock to my grandpa's house whenever we used to go for vacation.

"In a city, people do not have time for each other, not even for their neighbour. I've been reading in newspapers recently about deaths happening in one house and the other person coming to know about it only after a week – when the dead body starts to stink." The difference in these two social lives was quite stark.

I gave a call to my parents to confirm my safe arrival.

"Wash up and come for lunch," my *Guru's* wife instructed.

What should I call her? I wondered. I had heard that in the olden days, when students used to go and stay in the *Gurukul,* the *Guru* could also be a married person, not just a *Sannyasi.* The *Guru's* wife automatically became a mother for the students staying there.

*Guruma* was the way students would address her. It seemed apt for me too. So, along with my *Guru,* I had a *Guruma* here – a package deal of two in one!

My *Guruma* was no ordinary lady either. She herself was a Sanskrit scholar and held a PhD in the language, like her husband. It was my *Guru* who had inspired her to study further after their marriage. Their children were also highly educated and were pursuing corporate careers in the cities.

The village did not offer many opportunities for the highly educated, ambitious and career-oriented youth. This scholarly couple could have easily migrated to any city, but loved to have the best of both worlds.

They stayed in their village, but also travelled for many seminars and conferences. The Sanskrit books and research articles they wrote had worldwide readership. And therefore, they were invited to various countries to present their ideas in other universities.

My concept of a very poor and sober village man, who taught Sanskrit because he had no other option, changed dramatically over our lunch discussions. To stay back in the village was a conscious choice that he had made.

"When you called the first time to come here, I was not sure about taking you on as a student because of my hectic travel schedules." He was referring to that silent pause in our first conversation over the phone.

"Then why did you decide to accept me as your student?" I was curious.

"When I asked what inspired you to study the *Arthashastra*, you mentioned that your grandpa had created the interest. That touched my heart." Okay, so this was an emotional connect.

"You know, we have a grandson who stays abroad with my son and daughter-in-law," he smiled, looking at his wife. "Whenever we go there to spend time with our grandson, he always likes to listen to ancient Indian stories. During the last visit, I had told him the story of Chanakya… "

I almost knew what he was going to say next.

"I told him about Kautilya's *Arthashastra*, but that tiny

tot's little mind could not take more than Chanakya's story."
*Guruji* had already planted the seed which would sprout into
a tree at the right time, break ground at the right time to come.

Was it history repeating itself in a different family? This
tradition of passing on cultural values from grandparents to
grandchildren continues forever, I think – in every family, in
every generation.

"But the bigger reason to accept you as a student was your
acceptance to come here and study for six months. I was happy
to see your commitment. Few people from the cities do that."
My heart filled with joy on receiving this recognition of being
a committed student. I liked it.

"Okay, let's agree on the study format for the next six
months."

"Let him take a nap first. The poor child has travelled from
so far," my *Guruma* said to her husband.

# 15

# The Rules

I wanted to take a short nap, as suggested by *Guruma,* and be ready for my first set of instructions. I did not know that the journey had worn me out so much that by the time I woke up, it was almost sunset. Looking out of the window, I saw that it was getting dark and I felt very guilty.

I cursed myself: Is this why you have come here? To sleep? What a way to start your first class. Your *Guru* is waiting for you and you are sleeping like there's no tomorrow.

I hurried to the place where my *Guruji* was sitting. There were some people sitting around him. He beckoned to me when he saw me rushing towards him.

"This is the boy I was talking about. He has come all the way from the city to study the *Arthashastra,*" he proudly told some visitors.

While conversing with them, I discovered that these visitors were organizing some Sanskrit seminar, where my *Guru* was supposed to be a speaker.

"I will surely come. You can go ahead with the preparations and print the invitation cards with my name." The organizers were extremely happy and satisfied with those words. They got what they wanted – his time and approval.

He added, "I am not travelling out of town for the next six months at least. This boy has come all the way from the city and I need to spend quality time with him. Plus, I have just retired from the university. Let me spend some time with myself. Since yours is a local program and I don't have to travel, I will be there."

Looking at me proudly, he said to others, "The usual trend is people from villages want to study in cities and those who live in the cities want to study abroad. How many times have you heard of someone who will come from a city to a village to study?" I now knew the softer aspects he liked about me.

"Bring him for the program as well," requested the senior organizer.

"Of course, he will be there. I will make sure he comes along." Did I have a choice not to go?

As we all walked to the gate to see off the group, its youngest member came closer to me and whispered, "You are very lucky that he has accepted you as a student." I knew I was lucky, but what he said next was really humbling:

"I did my PhD under him. He was my guide. It took nearly four years of patient waiting for him to accept me. And in the next four years during my research, I never got to spend as much time with him as you will be able to." Was this person envious of me or was he bragging about being a student of *Guruji* even before I arrived on the horizon?

"I used to get just about half an hour every week with him and you will be getting his full attention for the next six months, that too on a daily basis. Thank your stars, thank your stars," he said, while disappearing in the distance with the others.

"Let me have a look at your *Arthashastra* book," *Guruji* wanted to know what I had read so far.

I showed him the book that grandpa had studied and passed on to me. It had his notes and mine in the same book. I also had a separate notebook. This contained the questions that had cropped up in my mind regarding the *Arthashastra* over the years. I needed answers for them as well.

"This is a good version of the *Arthashastra*. The translation in English is also good. Keep this as your primary book for studying over the next six months." I felt nice that I did not have to start all over again.

"But you need to read different versions of the *Arthashastra,* written by other scholars, to get different viewpoints. Never limit your knowledge to one person or one book. Keep your mind wide open."

As I was making mental notes, he continued: "Let's make a daily timetable for you for the next six months." He had already planned one. "You will stay in this ashram close to my house. It is no ordinary ashram. It is also a research centre of Indology studies recognized by the central government. It is a world class library with many rare books." Yes, I was already aware about this aspect of the ashram.

"I am on their advisory board and part of their research committee. We are a group of scholars from across the globe, working towards the revival of ancient Sanskrit books." I was getting introduced to Indology for the first time.

"The ashram atmosphere will also help you develop spiritually during your stay here. You come to my house every day from the ashram and we will have a class. I will tell you more about the study pattern tomorrow," he smiled. I think he understood that I required some time to settle down with his instructions.

"Tonight, you stay here only. Early morning, we will have a Ganesh Pooja and start your studies formally." Yes, Lord Ganesha was invoked before every activity to eliminate problems that may come while on the journey towards one's goal. He guarantees success.

My *Guru* was both a traditional and modern man. He believed in rituals, but also knew the significance and logic behind them. Later, he also taught me the logic of spirituality.

Touching my shoulders, he allowed me to retire for the day, "Tomorrow, you will be reborn... "

# 16

# The Initiation

I made sure I woke up before sunrise the next day. The house was already buzzing with activity. Both *Guruji* and *Guruma* were up. I could hear some noise in the kitchen. I took a bath and after getting ready, I slowly peeped into the hall, wondering what their daily routine was.

"Come on, let's do the pooja first." I saw my *Guruji* waiting for me. He took me to a small room, where a small temple had been set up. It had photos of various gods. The lamp was already lit. The Ganesha idol was placed in the centre.

"Lord Ganesha is the god of knowledge. He was the stenographer of Veda Vyasa, the author of the *Mahabharata* and the compiler of the *Vedas*," he told me of the philosophical aspect of Lord Ganesha. "If it were not for Ganesha's documentation, we would not have been able to keep all the ancient wisdom for generations to come."

He made me sit on a mat. Putting the sandal paste on my forehead and chanting a few mantras, he offered his prayers. He also asked me to offer my prayers along with him. Next, he took my copy of the *Arthashastra* and placed it in front of the lord. Putting some flowers on it, he said, "Now, think of not only Lord Ganesha, but also your *Gram Devata*, other gods, your forefathers, your parents and all other well-wishers."

As I closed my eyes to visualize each of them, he said, "Seeking their blessings to complete your studies with full concentration and devotion."

He then took a *Rudraksha Mala* from a drawer and placed it in front of Lord Shiva, whose idol was placed near Lord Ganesha's. He chanted some mantras. He then placed the *Rudraksha Mala* in my hands and said, "This *Rudraksha Mala* is from Kailash Manasarovar. I got it during my last visit there. It's come from a divine place." I took the *Mala* and touched it respectfully to both my closed eyes.

"It has 108 beads." I knew that it was a spiritual number as many people used these kind of *Malas*. "You should chant the *Gayatri* mantra everyday using this *mala*," he instructed. It meant that I had to chant the Gayatri mantra 108 times. This mantra is supposed to bring brilliance to one's intellect.

In the olden days too, the *Gayatri* mantra was used to initiate students into formal education. I was lucky to be initiated in this manner. Then, pointing at the rising sun, he said, "Then, pray to *Surya Bhagwan*. He is very powerful indeed, He is the source of all knowledge.

Remember, consider your study of the *Arthashastra* as your sadhana. Seek the grace of god at every step. There will be times when your studies may get boring or tiring, but complete every task with dedication." The attitude of studying was important, he told me.

I sat down quietly in front of him and chanted the *Gayatri* mantra using the *Rudraksha Mala* and prayed to the sun god. A small *Aarti* was then performed and I took my *Guruji* and *Guruma's* blessings by touching their feet.

"Breakfast is ready," my *Guruma* announced. There was something special about breakfast that day – it was not just tasty, but divine. It was the best *prasad* I had ever tasted. While eating, I asked my *Guruji*: "What is the meaning of Indology?"

"It is the study of all sciences of Indian origin. Like Vedic mathematics, Ayurveda, *Natyashastra*... even your study of the *Arthashastra* is considered a part of Indological studies." Later on, I came to know that the word 'Indology' was coined in western academic circles as a branch of studies related to anything and everything to do with India – its culture, tradition, literature, etc.

"Most of the scholars of Indology are not Indians," he informed me. I was not sure if I should feel happy or sad about it. Happy, because Indian knowledge was appreciated and being researched abroad, but sad, for we did not give much importance to our own wisdom.

I felt hopeful when my *Guru* continued, " ... but it is changing. A lot of Indians are taking keen interest in Indology."

Now being formally called a student of Indology, I felt nice. "Students like you have to study Indian wisdom and make it relevant for modern times."

I could see the bigger problem he was trying to address. "One issue with ancient Indian knowledge is the relevance to our present generation. No doubt, Indians are proud of their heritage, but when it comes to application, we fail. This is where other countries have an advantage."

Comparing India with other nations, he said, "Look at countries smaller and newer than ours; they have progressed faster than us. And here, in spite of so much intellectual work that has happened in the past, we are still struggling for survival." I was listening to him. I could also feel his pain.

"We only glorify our past. We need to study and research our ancient scriptures and bring solutions to modern-day problems. Looking into the past, we need to work in the present for a glorious future. We need to reinvent our own country, our own wisdom."

His agenda was handed over to me…

# 17

# A Walk in the Ashram

The ashram was a 20-minute walk from my *Guruji's* place. "Today, let us walk to the ashram. You will become familiar with the roads. There are also buses that can help you reach faster. Just check the bus timings," he instructed.

As we were walking, many people stopped to look at us on the way. They exchanged greetings with my *Guruji*. I remembered what he had told me, "In a village the first person knows the last person." The conversations also indicated that all of them knew about my coming to study under him. Yes, I was feeling safe and at home.

As we entered the gate of the ashram, the security guard saluted my *Guruji*. Some other workers also came over to him and paid their salutations. The ashram was spread over a few acres of land. He first took me to a small temple inside. "This temple has been here for ages. We were told stories of this temple as children. It is said that those who are blessed here become carriers of knowledge across different parts of the world.

But it had been neglected for many, many years, till a few years ago when this temple deity appeared in the dream of a wealthy businessman. The deity instructed him to rebuild this temple."

I was getting more interested in the story now, "When that businessman came here, he not only revived this temple but decided to make this place a centre of learning. Over the years, many people came to support his cause. Today, this has become a world-renowned centre for the study of Indology."

He then took me to the administrative office. Showing the photo of that wealthy and noble businessman, he said, "His son is a trustee of this ashram and continues to generate funds for all the research work that is done here. Even though he is a busy businessman, he is very involved in all the activities that take place here. Come, let's meet him."

I somehow did not have a good impression of wealthy men. They cheated the whole world to make money for themselves. Businessmen only knew how to give bribes and cheat the government.

As soon as I was introduced to him, he looked into my eyes and said, "Good, you have come here to study the Kautilya's *Arthashastra*." He had already been briefed, like everyone else, about my coming here to study the book.

"You know, there is a general impression that, Kautilya's *Arthashastra* is meant only for kings and for the proper rule of a kingdom in the olden days. This is not true, it can be used by anyone, during any time period, to solve any problem in any field."

He said these words with so much authority and conviction, that they just struck me like lightning!

"The *Arthashastra* has helped me become a successful businessman."

My goodness, what was he talking about? Business and

Arthashastra? As these questions popped one after another in my head, a young man appeared on the scene. This young man was handling the accounts and administration of the ashram. My *Guruji* told him, "Take him around the ashram and show him around." My *Guruji* and the trustee businessman then sat down for a serious discussion regarding some research work they had undertaken on Indology.

I was shown the various sections of the ashram and introduced to the other people working there. He took me to the administrative area, the kitchen, the dining room, hostel area for research scholars and also the fields where some vegetables were grown.

There were also a few monks in orange robes. "These are the *Sannyasis* of various spiritual organizations. They, too, come here to study and carry out their spiritual practices. This place is also considered as a spiritual retreat."

Then he took me to a large building. "This is the nucleus of this place – the library... people from all over the world come here to discover the books written centuries ago."

The moment I hear the word 'library', I get transported to a world of books. I feel at home when I'm in a library... any library. I feel I belong there, like it's my home.

The very size of the library impressed me. "There are over 1,00,000 books on Indology here," he said with pride.

"One lakh books?" Wow, that number was a dream come true for a young boy like myself who loved books.

"No, 1,00,000 books on Indology alone," he clarified. "We get many books here, but are selective about what we keep. Many donors give us books on various subjects, but we are clear that we only keep books on Indology. The rest are not kept here." It was then that I understood why it was called a centre for Indological research, a highly specialized field in academic studies.

He pointed to a corner, "You see that place? That table is reserved for you." This was the research scholar's section. It was like an individual cell. Serious scholars were allocated a table where they could take their books and make notes.

"No one is allowed to come and disturb a research scholar in those sections. Many people consider it a place of meditation." I felt proud that I was considered a research scholar here! If only my college friends were around to witness my achievement.

I had only one question, "Who runs this place? How do they ensure it is so well maintained and so divine?'

His answer was, "There are many people who run this place, but the backbone is the trustee whom you just met. He is a noble man. A role model businessman."

"Noble businessman? Can such a combination exist?" I asked skeptically.

"Do you want to know his story?" he enquired.

"Of course" I said.

"Let's go to the dining hall. I will tell you over a cup of tea."

# 18

# An Accountant with a Difference

The kitchen was full of activity. They were getting ready for lunch. About a hundred people had food here every day.

I was introduced to the kitchen in charge, "He will be staying here for the next six months. He is the *Arthashastra* research scholar from the city you were informed about."

He then turned to me and said, "These cooks are from the village around the ashram. The ashram gives them employment and they are all dedicated to this place. They are now more like family." There was a sense of pride in all of them.

Taking a cup of tea each, both of us sat on a dining table, facing each other. "Tell me more about your trustee – the noble businessman," I may have sounded a bit cynical in my tone. I think my ashram tour guide had sensed it too.

"It is not necessary that every wealthy man should be a crook," I wanted to get his view on the same. "I, too, used to think like you do. Later, on meeting the many people who come here, I realized if wealthy people take care of noble projects, they become noble automatically."

"Why would any wealthy businessman support a noble cause?" I asked. "I think it is because they like to have their names displayed all over the place. You see, all over various temples, churches, mosques and other religious places and organizations, the donors are given special privileges and their names are displayed in bold letters. They just want all that popularity. That is why they donate."

With a smile, he made his view on the topic known, "Yes, that is true to some extent, but to decide this as the only reason why rich people donate is not right. I have been working as an accountant in this ashram for the last 20 years. I know the source of funds to the ashram, who gives them and what amount. And you will be surprised to know that the maximum people who donate here insist that their names not be known to others. They want to keep it a secret.

I am not saying that donors' names are not displayed, or should not be displayed in the projects that they support, that is a different issue. What is important is that you keep an open mind about wealth and wealthy people. Kautilya's *Arthashastra* is also called a scripture on wealth. During your studies here, you will come to know the different ways in which wealth operates in the world."

My goodness! Even this accountant is quoting the *Arthashastra*! I was shocked. What kind of people am I meeting here? First that trustee speaks about *Arthashastra*, now this accountant is quoting the *Arthashastra*... who is next? The cook and the security guard? I was going off balance.

"Have you studied Kautilya's *Arthashastra*?" I asked him.

"Not like you are going to study here, but yes, I know quite a bit about this great book," he said with pride. "Your *Guru*, the person who has brought you here, is a great man. He is an expert on the *Arthashastra*. World-renowned scholars come here to clear their doubts in understanding the book." Yes, I knew he was an expert.

"One day our noble trustee said to him," he shot me a sarcastic smile as he said this, since he figured out that I did not like him being called noble. "Sir, so many people come here from all over the world to understand more about Kautilya's *Arthashastra*, but why don't you share the wisdom with us as well.' And *Guruji* had agreed to the request. He gave a series of lectures introducing us to Kautilya's *Arthashastra*."

"Who do you mean by 'us'?" I wanted to know.

"The ashram inmates, the trustees, the administrative staff, etc. Actually it began with us, but later on other people from the surrounding villages also joined the group, till finally about a hundred people were attending."

I became more curious. "How long were these lectures?"

"It was a 30-day lecture series on the overview of the *Arthashastra*. It was for one and a half hours every day after office hours. During those days, your *Guruji* was working for the university and could only give lectures after work. So, we all agreed to evening sessions."

He became nostalgic: "It was a daily *Satsang* for all of us. We learnt about Chanakya – the person, his life, the *Arthashastra* and its 6,000 sutras. The other works by Chanakya or credited to Chanakya, like *Laghu Chanakya*, *Rajneeti Shashtra*, *Chanakya Niti*, *Chanakya Sutras* and the other *Arthashastras* that came before Kautilya's and many, many more."

"What? There are other books on the *Arthashastra* apart from Kautilya's?" I did not know this.

"Fourteen *Arthashastras* had been written before Chanakya's, and many more have been written after that." Well, well, the accountant was quite a teacher himself. He soon realized that he should stop now and continue to be a good tour guide of the ashram, instead of showing off the knowledge he had acquired.

"But you are a lucky young man. None of us have studied here in the format you are about to adopt – six months of focused and detailed study of the *Arthashastra* through one-on-one teaching," he tried to be humble. "Okay, now let me show you the room where you will be staying," he directed me to a nearby passage.

I wanted to know more: "Are there any notes available from the lectures you had been given?"

"Yes, one of our Indology students at that time used to take daily notes of *Guruji's* lectures. Later on, all the notes he had taken were converted into a short book. It is available in the library," he pointed back towards the place where I could gather this wisdom.

"But if you really want to know how to practice the *Arthashastra* in real life, then meet our trustee and discuss its application in today's world with him," he smiled.

"Our trustee is a living embodiment of Kautilya's *Arthashastra* – he is rich from the outside as well as inside."

# 19

# The Noble Businessman

We went back to the room where *Guruji* and the trustee were sitting.

"Sir, I have showed him the place, as requested," said the accountant to the trustee. It is strange, but I no longer wanted him to be referred to as a trustee anymore; I now quite liked the terms 'noble businessman' together. If the phrase was indeed true, I would like to be one myself someday.

What? I thought to myself. Now, I want to be a businessman, too?

How did this come to be? As a young boy who had just graduated, I had never thought of my career and the life ahead. This was the case with most of the young boys of our generation, too. None of us were clear about what we wanted in life. We just grabbed at every opportunity that came our way.

I said to myself, if a businessman can be noble and it can be a platform to practice the *Arthashastra,* then why not? But I wanted to know more about this from Mr. Noble Businessman himself.

"I hope you like the place," he said to me, but again sounded like a trustee who was happy to showcase his ashram to a new visitor.

"I hope you will feel comfortable in the room allocated to you during your days here." He was ensuring that I was well taken care of, so that I would feel at home.

"If there are any problems, there are many people around here to help you out," he assured me.

Then, he looked back at *Guruji* and picked up their conversation from where they had left off, "Yes sir, you are right. It is important to pay taxes for the larger good of society. Even though the *Arthashastra* talks about corruption in the government, it points to a *Dharmic* society." They were deliberating upon a more profound topic.

"Okay, we will discuss this later in more detail. I have a few more questions," he concluded.

*Guruji* turned to me. "Okay, now you can settle yourself comfortably in the ashram. I am going home now; I have a little writing work to do. I will see you at my home tomorrow. Enjoy." With these words, he left.

I stood alone with the noble businessman. "So, what prompted you to study Kautilya's *Arthashastra?*" he asked casually.

"My grandfather." I had to repeat the entire story again. I began to feel like I was either a unique person who had taken up an entirely new study or a person who did not know why he was doing it.

"The book helped me as a businessman," he said frankly.

This was exactly what I wanted to ask him about. "How?" I prompted him to go on.

"Most of the time, when you study *Shastras* or scriptures, you do not have clarity on  their real-life application. The wisdom of these words come alive during critical moments and challenges in life. The *Arthashastra* did that for me."

His words were to guide me in the face of challenges that were yet to come.

"I have been lucky to be born with a silver spoon in my mouth – into a business family; not just a wealthy family, but a wealthy family with values."

Remembering his father, he said, "My father spent a lot of his money on spiritual causes. One of these projects was this ashram, where he wanted to revive ancient Indian scriptures."

"Tell me more." I was keen that he continue his story.

"When he built this place, apart from simply spending money on it, he went to different parts of India, collecting various manuscripts that were valued just as much. There are many rare, untapped books in this place. We invite scholars like you to study them and rediscover them for our generation.

I, too, had a taste for ancient books like you, but the real journey starts after you complete the study. Whenever I did my business, for every challenge I faced, I picked up the *Arthashastra* and always found the solutions within its pages."

"For example?" I sought clarity.

"For example, the *Arthashastra* deals with various topics like identification of wealth, creation of wealth, management of wealth and distribution of wealth. So, I knew very well that I needed to identify where wealth would come from before I could create it. At the same time, I need not just create or manage wealth; I should also give back to the society that I got it from." I was truly impressed.

"The *Arthashastra* also helps you with problems, such as how to recruit your managers, how to collaborate with different partners and how to deal with competition in the market place."

As he spoke, a roadmap of my life was being sketched in my mind.

"Sir, I have absolutely no direction in my life as to what I should do and how I should go about doing it. But now, one thought that comes to my mind is... " I hesitated, "that I, too, would like to be a businessman." I wanted to see whether he liked the idea or not.

"Brilliant! There is nothing like being a noble businessman, who positively contributes to the society."

"How do I become one?" I asked eagerly.

"Don't worry about that. First, study the *Arthashastra*. The path you should take will automatically open up to you," he smiled.

That day, for the first time in my life, I had finally found an answer to the question everyone had been asking of late: "What do you want to do in life?"

"A businessman with a difference," I would say to them proudly.

The *Arthashastra* was to show me the way forward.

# 20

# The Study Pattern

I woke up the next morning, unsure of how the ashram routine worked. Even before sunrise, activities were on in full swing. I could hear the temple bells ringing, some chanting Vedic hymns while breakfast was being prepared in the kitchen.

I got ready and went to the temple. The *Pujari* there was performing the *Aarti* when I reached. Taking the *Prasad*, I walked around the ashram just to get a feel of the new place where I would be putting up for the next six months.

This was all amounting to an entirely fresh, new experience for me. The birds chirped gleefully as the villagers carried on with their daily duties. There was no one here like my mother to wake me up and tell me that breakfast was ready.

After some time, a bell rang in the kitchen, indicating that it was time for breakfast. I walked towards the dining hall and joined the few others who had come there.

I started making friends with everyone as I knew I would need their help and support over the next few months. After all, these people were my new family.

I went to my room and picked up the *Arthashastra* and my notebook. I then walked into the library and kept my books in the study corner that had been allotted to me. The librarian gave me a warm smile, "Take a look around the library and you will find some other books on the *Arthashastra* here."

I took his advice and examined the carefully selected books that were kept so neatly in the library. Then I went to the section named *Arthashastra*.

There were over 200 books in this section. They were each written by different scholars. Some were translations, some were notes, some were lecture series compiled into a book and some were the proceedings of seminars. Some books were thin with just 30-odd pages, while others were huge commentaries.

I was happy to see so many different books on my subject. I also found a copy of the same *Arthashastra,* which my grandfather had handed down to me.

Then, I found a copy of the book named *Introduction to Arthashastra*. This was the same book that the accountant had informed me about – the compilation of the lectures my *Guru* had given to the ashram's members.

I felt at home, while going through these various books. I wandered into other sections too and looked at the numerous manuscripts on various subjects. Some of these were written on palm leaves and others had even been written on cloth!

"You can pick up any book and take it to your study table," said the librarian, who was hovering around me to make sure I got as much help as possible.

Not knowing where to begin, I felt a bit overwhelmed by the pool of knowledge available in this divine place. Even if I wanted, I would not be able to read all these books in one lifetime, I thought to myself.

I returned to my table, closed my eyes and asked god to guide me on the path ahead.

Then, I opened my own copy of the *Arthashastra* and began reading it.

The opening verse on the very first page was a solemn prayer:

*Om Namah Sukra Brahaspati Bhyam...*

I was trying to understand the meaning of this verse. Who were Sukra and Brahaspati? I got hold of some other reference books and found out that Sukra was the *Guru* of the Asuras, while Brahaspati was the *Guru* of the *Devas*.

Why would Chanakya pray to two *Gurus* at the same time? I wondered. I made a note of the same, wanting to seek clarity on it from my *Guru*.

I passed quite a few hours in the library, making many such personal notes on the *Arthashastra*. I had taken a short break during lunch time, after which I resumed my study.

Then, as discussed with *Guruji,* I went to his house towards the end of the day.

He was waiting for me. "So, what did you do today?"

"I tried to gather maximum information about the other *Arthashastra* books available in the library," I announced, not without a hint of pride.

"What was your conclusion?"

I said, "There are plenty of books on the subject. I would like to read as many of them as possible and do a cross comparison. Also, I would like it if you could help me understand anything I find unclear."

"This is a good pattern of study. You read the books and what you have not understood, we will discuss and clarify together.

An ideal student, according to our tradition, is the one who comes prepared," he was evidently pleased with me.

"Most students just come, open their books in front of the teacher and expect to be spoon-fed with the knowledge contained in their pages.

"So, your pattern of studying the *Arthashastra* will be like this: you read each verse of various books, do a comparative study and then come to me. I will clear whatever doubts remain."

"By studying one chapter of the *Arthashastra* a day, you will be able to complete the full book in six months comfortably." This average target that had just been set was reasonable.

"So, what doubts do you bring to me today?" he asked.

I read from the notes I had taken in the library, "Sir, why does Chanakya pray to both Sukra and Brahaspati at the same time. Don't they contradict one another?"

"Let me explain..." he began.

# 21

# Different Views – Your View

To know any subject in detail, you should know its background, such as why it was born.

"The *Arthashastra* has many meanings. It is popularly known as the science of politics, but political science is an all inclusive science. It includes economics, social science, law, arts, etc," *Guruji* explained. "The best way to study any subject is to know what the previous teachers or experts had done in that field. This will not only give you a historical perspective, but also enlighten you about various viewpoints. Both Sukra and Brahaspati were teachers of the *Arthashastra,* meaning the science of politics." This, I did not know.

"Therefore, Chanakya bows before all the previous acharyas before writing his own version of the *Arthashastra,* known as 'Kautilya's *Arthashastra'.*"

"Are the *Arthashastras* of Sukra and Brahaspati available to us?" I asked.

"They were lost with time, but you never know; if you properly research all the manuscripts available to us, you may find them in some corner of India, the way Kautilya's *Arthashastra* was found."

"Kautilya's *Arthashastra* was *found*? When? Where?" I had assumed that this treasure was something that had been systematically written and passed down through the generations. I didn't know it had been lost and then rediscovered!

"Many years ago, a Sanskrit scholar named Shyama Shastry was rearranging the various old Sanskrit manuscripts available in Mysore University. In this process, he suddenly came across Kautilya's *Arthashastra*." I could see the glint of joy in *Guruji's* eyes, as he narrated the story.

"He hit a jackpot by chance!" What a treasure he had unearthed for us!

"He was so happy with the discovery that he translated the book into English himself, which led to its popularity in the English-speaking countries as well." Ah, so that was how the book got translated into so many foreign languages.

"But, do you know what?" *Guruji's* excitement was far from over. "He arranged all the remaining manuscripts, categorized them and kept them safe for generations to come. He was a great curator. You can still go and find manuscripts on various other subjects in that library." I made up my mind to go there at some point in my life.

Coming back to the prayer Chanakya had offered to Sukra and Brahaspati, he explained that the prayer has a deeper significance.

"The *Arthashastra* is also known as *Rajniti Shastra*. Both Sukra and Brahaspati were *Gurus*. At different points in history, we find that both these *Gurus* had given contradictory advice to their respective students. They addressed issues differently." Same topic, different views!

"Chanakya had studied all the *Arthashastras* before he wrote his own. So, irrespective of what these *Gurus* said, he humbly bowed before them in respect and accepted their views with an open mind. In fact, Chanakya, in various places, has a different opinion himself, totally at odds with those from previous teachers."

Well, I liked the idea of having your own perspective on any subject and not just blindly following what others believe.

"So, what does this teach you?" *Guruji* asked me.

"I think, it's best to learn from earlier teachers, even if they have contradictory views – and to take your own independent stand," I concluded.

"Brilliant," *Guruji* was happy. He added, "Also, never belittle previous teachers and their wisdom, just because you feel it is outdated. Respect all teachers. That is the real message." He wanted me to note this down in particular.

"How can you apply what you have just learnt in your personal life?" he quizzed.

I did not think I would face such a question. I realized that my *Guru* was far more interested in the *Arthashastra's* practical application.

"Practical application in which field?" I wanted some sort of direction to think in.

"In any field. The learnings of *Arthashastra* can be used in any situation or profession," he said.

"Even in business?" I was hazarding a guess of sorts.

"Of course. As I said before, it can be applied in any field," he repeated.

I started visualizing myself as a businessman and thought about a situation where I would have to use this prayer.

Gathering my thoughts, I tried building this story: "Suppose that I am sitting in my office and two of my employees are having a fight. I will call both of them to my cabin and listen to both of them. I will take both their viewpoints into account."

*Guruji* was listening with interest. "And then?"

"And then, I will use my own judgment to assess the situation. Even though I will listen to both of them individually, I will not get carried away by their views. I will have my own stand, my own logic," I summed up.

"Brilliant. Very good," he said happily.

He tested me further by creating another situation: "What if you are their boss and you have to decide who is right between them. What will you do?"

"I will not get emotional about the situation and take a decision, which is in the larger interest of my organization. I will try to be a good judge and take the right call." I found myself thinking deeply and clearly.

"Now you have already started thinking like a leader. Remember, one of the qualities of a good leader is to be a good judge of situations and take the right decisions," *Guruji* advised.

"Tomorrow, we will think in more detail about how to think correctly."

"Thinking about thinking?" I asked confused.

"Yes, the Chanakya way – it's called *Aanvikshiki*." Yes, I had heard that word before.

"The first book of *Arthashastra* is called *Vinayadhikarikam*, and the topic dealt with is *Vidyyasammudesah*. In that, Chanakya starts with *Aanvikshiki Sthapana*. Read about *Aanvikshiki* and come. We will discuss it in detail tomorrow."

That night when I retired to bed, I was a different person.

For a change, I was actually thinking!

# 22

# Thinking – A Gift to Human Beings

I was very fresh when I arose in the morning. There was something very different about the day. Was it because it was very beautiful outside? Was it because I had now settled down in the ashram after the initial anxiety of adjusting to new surroundings? Or was it that something had changed deep down within me?

As suggested by *Guruji,* I spent that day reading the first chapter of the *Arthashastra – Aanvikshiki Sthapana.* There was something about that chapter and that word – *Aan-vik-shi-ki.* It was mysterious and also gripping, yet, not fully understood.

I looked up the commentary on it in various books by other scholars. There were numerous translations. *Aanvikshiki* meant philosophy, *Bhramavidya,* spiritual knowledge, logical thinking, etc.

But that day, I wanted to know what *Guruji's* take on this would be. The knowledge of the *Arthashastra* starts with the sutra:

*Aanvikshiki, Trai, Vaarta, Dandaniti cheti Vidya* (1.2.1)

"A king or leader is required to possess four types of knowledge – *Aanvikshiki* (philosophy), *Trai* (Vedas), *Vaarta* (economics) and *Dandaniti* (political science)," *Guruji* translated. "Once he understands these four types of knowledge, the leader will be very efficient and productive. Each of these has been explained in detail in the *Arthashastra*. But the most important is *Aanvikshiki*," he stressed.

"*Guruji*, why is it so important?" I added this to my list of questions.

"Chanakya himself explains the concept in the same chapter:

*Aanvikshiki is ever thought of as the lamp of all sciences, as the means of all actions and as the support of all laws and duties.* (1.2.12)

It is a guiding force," my *Guru* emphasized. "Thinking is the very foundation of any activity, the basis on which human beings develop from one generation to another.

*Aanvikshiki* is best translated as the science of thinking. And thinking is nature's gift to human beings. They are endowed with a very useful asset called the 'intellect'. This is what makes us the crown of all of god's creations." Yes, *I think, therefore, I am.*

"But the most surprising part is that human beings do not like to think at all," *Guruji* said sadly.

"Why do we not like to think?" I wanted to know.

"Thinking takes a lot of energy. Scientific research has also proven that it is not easy to think logically. It is a very exhausting activity. It can lead to fatigue. Man likes to take the easy path.

Why waste all that energy? Best not to think at all, right? But surprisingly, human beings have progressed only because of thinkers – the thought leaders. They ask difficult questions and seek difficult answers. They break the status quo."

I asked, "So, what we require is to ensure thinking for progress and development? And that is what *Aanvikshiki* is all about?"

"Not just thinking, but the right thinking, philosophical thinking in particular," He clarified.

"*Aanvikshiki* is about alternative thinking, lateral thinking, thinking out of the box. But, it is also about questioning if there is a box at all." So many dimensions!

"Just thinking is not enough; it has to be based on *Dharma* – righteousness." Now, I had started understanding a little bit about why *Aanvikshiki* was also called philosophy.

"Even without the base of philosophy and spirituality, you can still think and create new objects, but you may cause a lot of harm to other human beings and the environment in doing so," *Guruji* said gravely.

"Is that the reason Chanakya explains *Aanvikshiki* at the very beginning of the *Arthashastra*?" I asked.

"Yes, this philosophical thinking is the very foundation on which a leader is created by Chanakya. After all, he wanted to create a *Raja-Rishi*, a philosopher king or a sage-like king."

"*Guruji*... *Aanvikshiki* is a unique word. Was it invented by Chanakya?" I had been curious about this for a while now.

"No, no. This is not a new word at all. You will find *Aanvikshiki* all over ancient Indian books – in the *Mahabharata*, *Shrimad Bhagawatam* and in a lot of Sanskrit literature. It is quite a popular word among Sanskrit scholars. *Aanvikshiki* existed even before Chanakya." My goodness! Such a famous word, yet none of the people I knew were aware of this.

The discussion suddenly took a different turn.

*Guruji* said, "By the way, do you know that one of Draupadi's names in the *Mahabharata* is *Aanvikshiki?*"

Really? "No, I did not know that," I admitted. I was then handed the names of some reference titles to study further.

"India has vast literature on the history of strategic thinking. Our ancestors were no ordinary people. They were men with brilliant intellect. We are all *Rishi-putras* – the children of great thinkers and spiritual giants. "

His explanation continued:

"*Aanvikshiki* is also known as *Brahma Vidya,* the ultimate knowledge of self-realization," he paused. "Therefore, you will find that we were successful spiritually and materially. *Aanvikshiki* teaches you to get worldly and spiritual success, both at one go. "

I took a break from asking any further questions. I was surprised and also shocked. From one word alone, *Guruji* had unlocked a sea of knowledge available in the *Arthashastra.* I was wondering what Chanakya had to say in the remaining books.

*Guruji* could read my face. "Enough for today. We have just started you on your journey to understanding Chanakya's way of thinking. There's a long way to go, " he said with sympathy.

I had stopped thinking, or had I just begun?

## 23

# Think, but Also Act

Iwas so engrossed in the thoughts of *Aanvikshiki* that I honestly felt a bit lost. I had never ever felt so absorbed in my own world. Time just flew by. I enjoyed being alone with my thoughts.

It is said that one should not feel lonely, but should enjoy being alone. I was alone, but I had connected with myself. I was thinking about thinking.

The next day, as I was studying the *Arthashastra*, I came across an interesting verse:

*An arrow, discharged by an archer, may or may not kill one person, or may not kill even one; but the intellect operated by a wise man would kill even children in the womb.* (10.6.51)

Sharpened intellect! I realized that this is what Chanakya wanted to teach the leaders – to use their intellect in the best possible manner. I was so inspired that I spent many hours together studying the *Arthashastra*.

I flipped through various chapters from beginning to end

and, for the first time, was impressed about the fact that the book spoke about various aspects of thinking.

When I went for my evening class, I asked, "*Guruji,* is it not that the *Arthashastra* – and *Aanvikshiki* in particular – teaches you how to use your intellect in full?"

"And also, where not to use your intellect," *Guruji* said matter-of-factly.

"Where not to use our intellect?" I was surprised and felt a bit deflated as well. I thought I had rightly concluded that it was about sharpening the intellect.

"One of the problems with intelligent people is that they do not stop thinking. They think so much that they do not act at all," he said.

"Analysis, analysis and only analysis leads to paralysis," he smiled. "Yes, you are right. The *Arthashastra* is about logical thinking, but the fact is that the most intelligent person also knows that there is something beyond the intellect and human understanding. You know, go to the sixth book of the *Arthashastra;* it talks about the qualities of a king or leader," he pointed to my copy.

I immediately took it in my hands and turned to the concerned page:

*"The excellences of the king are... intelligence and spirit."* (6.1.3)

He explained the verse to me in detail and made me visualize an ideal leader:

"An excellent leader is one who is intelligent and also dynamic (in spirit). Without dynamism and enthusiasm, a leader cannot energize others. And without energy, no one will work.

A leader is the one who *inspires*," he said with a force that I still cannot forget.

"Yes, it is important to think, but one should take the leap of faith when action has to be taken."

"But *Guruji*, how do we know how much to think and when to stop thinking?" I asked.

"Very good question. One needs to think and do, and also do and think. Thinking and taking action should happen simultaneously; both go hand-in-hand."

A great man once said, 'Plan out your work and work out your plan'.

After one has thought enough from all possible angles, one should jump into action. Without action, all plans are useless," was his advice.

"To stop thinking and take the leap of faith, one needs to have a strong spiritual foundation. A spiritual person knows when to think and when to act; you need to balance both."

"What if I do not have a spiritual foundation and I am a beginner on the spiritual path?" I wondered out loud.

"Simple; in such a situation, take advice from a spiritual *Guru*. Such a person will tell you to take action when required. You will find such guidance even today."

My mind wandered back to a discussion papa had had with a rich businessman, who had come to our house. I had overheard their conversation:

"How did you get into this line of business?" papa had asked.

"It was simple. My *Guru* told me to start the business and I just did it. I did not think too much after that and look how rich I have become! It's *Guru's* grace," the successful businessman had said with a laugh.

As my mind found its way back to the *Arthashastra,* I wondered about my ability to take decisions in such complex situations that may arise in the future.

"The kings always had *Raja-Gurus* on their side, who were their primary advisors," *Guruji* educated me about the system that operated in India in the olden days.

"The *Raja-Gurus* were the intelligent ones with a spiritual base. They knew what to do and when. All great kings became great because of their advisors and spiritual guides."

With every chapter that I studied, my *Guruji* made me think, think again and think some more.

Time just flew by and I suddenly realized that four months were over.

Just two more months to go? I suddenly remembered Time. And then I looked at the number of chapters of the *Arthashastra* that I had completed. I had not even done 50 percent!

Like a cricket batsman suddenly wanting to make more runs to increase his run rate, I started to put more efforts and more hours into my study. I was used to studying as much as 18 hours a day, now, and had managed to get a little grip on Sanskrit. Others in the ashram saw me sitting till late in the library and getting up early. I was pushing myself to complete my target of learning the 6,000 sutras in the six-month timeframe.

"There are many other ways of studying the *Arthashastra* than just reading in the library," said my *Guruji* quietly one day, as if he had witnessed my efforts.

"What are they?' I wanted to know.

"By meeting various experts on the *Arthashastra,*" he said.

"For the next two days, we will be going for a national conference on *Arthashastra.* There you will learn more from many."

# 24

# The Conference

I had woken up earlier than usual and met *Guruji*. A car had been arranged to pick him up and take him to the conference venue.

I recollected that the organizers were the people whom I had met on the first day at *Guruji's* house. They had come to invite him for this conference.

This two-day seminar had been organized at a national level with various people coming from across the country. There were scholars who were supposed to present papers on various topics from the *Arthashastra,* there were professors and teachers, students and even reporters.

We reached the venue before time. The state's chief minister came to inaugurate the conference. As the chief minister arrived, he was led to a VIP room for a cup of tea and an informal chat. My *Guruji* was the keynote speaker and a world-renowned expert on *Arthashastra* and it is there that I came to know that the chief minister had known him personally for his credentials and academic achievement. *Guruji* was also called to share that VIP room with the chief minister and other organizers.

"Come with me and stick with me, or you will get lost in

this crowd," he said in an authoritative tone. I, too, understood that if I did not follow *Guruji,* no one would allow me to even get close to the VIP room.

This was my first interaction with a politician in such close quarters. I felt as if I were in a dream. The people around seemed to be powerful and I could not understand some of their discussions at all. But what the chief minister told my *Guruji* left a lasting impression on me: "Sir, I was reading your article on Chanakya's thoughts for good governance. Can I request you to take a session for my cabinet ministers on the same topic?" *Guruji* agreed immediately and the chief minister's assistant was told to work out the details.

I was very proud of having a *Guru* who taught me the *Arthashastra,* but to know that he was also sought by powerful people like the chief minister was a matter of honour.

"Did I not tell you that you are a lucky boy?" The same person who had done his PhD under *Guruji's* guidance and whom I had met at *Guruji's* house whispered to me. I nodded and smiled. I now truly understood what he meant.

When the conference started with the inauguration ceremony, the dais was filled with prominent people. *Guruji* was sitting next to the chief minister. Speech after speech, the ceremony was full of praise for the *Arthashastra.* After the inaugural ceremony, the chief minister left and we had a tea break.

*Guruji* noticed that I was absolutely enchanted by the entire conference, but he also sensed that I was a bit lost in this congregation. He patted me on my back and said encouragingly, "Now the real study of the *Arthashastra* starts."

He took me aside, saying, "Now the media people have left along with the chief minister and the experts will speak on various dimensions of the *Arthashastra.* Make sure you learn from all of them. Develop your contacts and make friends. These will be helpful to you throughout life."

The technical paper presentations started, with various panelists speaking on different aspects of the *Arthashastra* – from philosophy to management, leadership, foreign policies and international affairs. We even had a military expert speaking.

Until this point, I thought that I was the only person who wanted to study the *Arthashastra,* but this conference humbled me. There are many out there, doing the same work, just in a different manner.

I remembered grandpa, who had once told me, "The *Arthashastra* is not the property of any particular person, nation or even generation. It's open to all those who want to understand the great Chanakya."

*Guruji* was right; listening to all these experts, I started understanding the *Arthashastra* through their various insights. It was a great learning experience.

I was introduced to various scholars, who spoke alongside *Guruji* and other organizers. They made sure I felt comfortable.

Over the next two days, I attended all the sessions, took notes, made sure I gathered whatever written material was available on the *Arthashastra,* developed contacts with scholars and even bought books on the *Arthashastra* that were displayed in the book exhibition.

I was also told that a book will be published based on all the presentations and proceedings of the conference. I booked a copy of the same too, so that it would then become a part of the collection in my library.

As the conference was ending, a young professor came to me. "Are you not the student who is learning the *Arthashastra* under *Guruji's* guidance?"

"Yes," I replied, still trying to figure out if I had interacted with him in the last two days. I was not sure.

"We are organizing a similar *Arthashastra* conference in our state in the near future. Would you kindly come and present your paper there?" he requested.

"Me?" I was startled and did not know how to react. "No, sir. I am just a beginner in this field. I am no scholar. I don't know as much as you all do. I am just a recent student of *Guruji's*."

"Just a student of *Guruji?*" he smiled. "That itself qualifies you to be a speaker for the next conference."

Even before I could utter another word, he said, "I will send you the details soon."

# 25

# The Final Days

Guruma asked, "So, are you not excited about going home?"

I realized I was in the last month of my studies. Good times go by fast. Yes, I wanted to meet my parents and friends. But, the thought that my *Gurukul* days were soon going to be over was saddening.

I also realized that I was lagging behind in meeting my daily target of *Arthashastra* verses. I still had almost 2,000 more verses to go. I did not want to leave any stone unturned in completing my studies on time. It was like running a marathon, only I was racing against time. I did nothing but study all day and spent sleepless nights, putting in more hours of research than usual.

On several occasions, I even suffered blackouts and often dozed off in the library. I had never worked so hard in my life. Now, I truly understood how bright, high-ranking students studied. I was determined to burn the midnight oil like them. The strain of it all reflected on my face.

"What happened to you?" *Guruji* looked concerned as I walked into his home one evening. "Why are you so dull and sleepy?"

"*Guruji*, I am studying day and night to complete my portion. I am redoubling my efforts as this is my last month here." I expected him to laud my dedication.

However, he did just the opposite. "Stop studying in this manner. Go and close your books and take a one-week break."

"Break?" I was not sure if I had heard him correctly.

"Don't overwork yourself. It will only worsen your ability to study effectively," he said. "There are many beautiful places around this village. In the last five months here, you have never seen any place apart from the ashram. Go and explore these natural surroundings yourself."

Those words were such a relief. The impact they had on me was akin to a rubber band, which had been suddenly released after being stretched to its limit.

*Guruma* and *Guruji* drew up a tourist plan, covering some ancient temples, mountains and seas nearby. They also called up a few friends and made arrangements for my stay in those places.

"Make sure you leave your *Arthashastra* book behind before you leave." That was *Guruji's* stern instruction, while *Guruma* looked on with a knowing smile. "Sometimes you have to let go of something to understand it better."

When I returned from the break, I felt like a recharged battery. I was ready to take up any challenge. With a few tips from *Guruji*, I completed the book almost one week in advance.

"Now, get ready for your test," *Guruji* announced. I was shocked! I had not come here to take another exam. I hated the kind of education system that tested a person's knowledge based on a three-hour question paper. Unfortunately, I could not argue against it; I had to follow his instructions without question.

"Okay, when will I have to attempt the question paper?" I asked, so that I could prepare accordingly.

"What question paper?" he mocked playfully. "Whatever you have studied of the *Arthashastra* in the last six months here, prepare a research paper based on that; that itself will show how well you have comprehended the subject." I took a deep breath and relaxed.

And thus, I wrote my first proper research paper on my understanding of the *Arthashastra*. I also gathered some inputs from research journals available in the library, so that it looked like some serious professional work. After all, I was now expected to be a scholar!

The day after I submitted my paper to *Guruji*, he called me.

"Very good work. I liked your thought process on the *Arthashastra* and how it can be applied in modern day businesses. It's a very unique approach." I had passed my test.

"Well done," he smiled. "Now your course is over. Make sure you take your certificate before you leave for home."

"Certificate?" I asked. Was it usual to get one?

"You are the first student of Indology, who has done systematic research on the *Arthashastra* in our ashram. We are recognized as a research institute by the central government, remember?" he explained.

"A few days ago, the trustee and I were discussing you and your commitment to your studies. We decided to give you a certificate for the course you have completed." This was nothing short of a windfall for me.

"In fact, a very senior monk scholar, who stays at the ashram, was also impressed by your commitment. He, too, suggested the same." Oh, I did not know that people in the ashram were observing my work so closely!

Then, in a more mellowed voice, he added, "You have been a brilliant student, the kind every teacher dreams of." I got a bit emotional when *Guruji* said this.

"This certificate will help you throughout your life," he continued. "It may seem like a piece of paper now, but it gives you the academic credentials that will take you forward by leaps and bounds. It's proof of your study of the *Arthashastra* here." It sounded as if *Guruji* could foresee things, that the young boy in me still could not.

"How much are the fees, sorry, I mean how much *Guru Dakshina* should I pay?" This was the last thing that I needed to address in order to close things at my end.

"No fees, only maintain your commitment to apply the *Arthashastra* in your life. Remember, *Shastras* have to be lived, not just learnt." Tears rolled down my cheeks as I heard these words.

On my last day at the ashram, I went up to the trustee and thanked him as well.

"Sir, I want to thank you and tell you something." He looked at me curiously. "I want to be like you – a noble businessman," I confessed. He said nothing, but simply smiled at me.

As I took my *Guruji* and *Guruma's* final blessings before heading to the bus stop, a small voice within me said, "Go conquer the world with your knowledge; you are ready now."

One chapter of my life had ended; another had just begun.

# 26

# The Homecoming

On board the train back to metropolitan life, I reflected on how I had lived my days so far. I thought of the past – my grandpa, my childhood interest in books, the urge to study the *Arthashastra* and then, studying the same in the *Gurukul* and *Guru Shishya* format.

My thoughts turned to my present situation – my mind was in a state of utter bliss. I had enjoyed myself thoroughly in the last six months, free from any anxiety about the future.

I was completely in tune with myself. The best part, I realized, was that I had done it all on my own without any expectations.

Finally, I began to think about the future. Once I reached home, the city's hectic lifestyle would surely claw at this blissful mental state of mine.

People would definitely ask me, "What are you going to do next?" I was not sure if I had an answer, but I wanted to choose my own path ahead in life, rather than letting the world decide it for me.

When I reached home, it felt as if a decade had passed. Many things had changed, though most things remained as they were before I left.

The curtains were different, but the furniture was the same. Many new books had been added to our collection, but the bookshelf itself was as familiar as it had always been.

Beaming that finally her son was back home, my mother hurriedly said, "Let's have lunch first." This reminded me of *Guruma;* she had said the same thing when I had first met her.

Papa asked, "So, how was the journey?" Was it *Guruji* asking me this question, I wondered. It took me a while to reconnect with the place I had left behind six months ago.

"Your friends were wondering where you had disappeared to," papa chuckled as he filled me in on my friends' queries while I had been away.

"You also missed quite a few family functions and festivals. Have a look at these photos," my mother chimed in with her share of stories.

Then, I started narrating my own experience. I told them about the kind of lifestyle I led, the ashram's divine ambience, the corner in the library that became my meditation cell, the way *Guruji* and *Guruma* had treated me during my stay, the visit to the conference where the chief minister was present and also, the unexpected invitation to speak at an upcoming conference.

Suddenly, papa's expression changed as if he had just remembered an important message for me. He said, "By the way, your graduation results came a few months ago. You got excellent marks. In fact, in one of the subjects, you even topped your college."

According to my father, this had been the best academic performance of my life. Somehow, it did not really excite me. I could have merely shrugged my shoulders and said, "So what?"

Instead, I slowly removed from my bag, the certificate that *Guruji* had issued to me for completing my Indology research course on the *Arthashastra*. I was more proud holding this in my hand than the certificate I had received from college.

Both my parents looked at it in surprise. Like me, they, too, had never imagined that I would come back with some academic certificate.

"That is a fantastic percentage, my dear son!" my mother was overjoyed.

"Percentage? What percentage?" I did not understand.

"Look, you got 92 percent and an A+ grade. It is given in the certificate."

I took a close look at the certificate. When *Guruji* had handed it to me, I had just checked for my name and the logo of the university with which our research institute was affiliated.

I did not know that it actually had my marks and grade printed as well. My score was based on certain criteria, which I was unaware of. I had unknowingly qualified as a research scholar. Now I realized why *Guruji* had called it a test.

"Wow, I never received such good marks in my life!"

The coincidence was even better. I had managed to earn excellent marks both in college as well as in the Indology research course I had just finished. Was this what they called *Guru Krupa, Ishwar Krupa* and *Shastra Krupa?*

"Your friends will be coming over in the evening. They had called," my mother informed.

I was not particularly keen on meeting my friends, but at the same time, I was curious to know what had happened in time that had elapsed since the last time we met.

When we met in the evening, we talked endlessly. One friend said he had never expected to clear the exams; another had just clinched his first job.

A girl had recently gotten engaged and was to get married in a few months, as if all her parents had waited for was for her to complete her graduation.

A few other friends were still looking for a job, while another had taken admission for further studies.

"What will you do now?" I knew this question was going to come straight at me.

I was now prepared with the answer: "I am going to be a businessman, an entrepreneur!"

They were surprised, because in the many years that we had been friends, I had never expressed such a desire. They probably thought it to be just another random passing thought of mine.

"I am serious, I want to be a businessman. I want to create wealth." I wanted to make sure they heard me out.

"What kind of business are you getting into?" one of them asked.

"A noble business," I said, remembering the trustee.

"Okay, fine, but what line of business?"

I really had no idea.

So, I started thinking...

# 27

# Astrology Shows the Way

O nce again, I sought papa's help.

"Papa, I want to be a noble businessman. I do not want to work under anyone. I want to be my own boss," I began, while my father listened patiently.

"All that is fine, but, my son, you should be clear about which business you want to get into." Papa tried to nudge me into sketching a more detailed plan, but I replied thoughtlessly:

"The kind of business that will make me rich, very rich?"

Papa pretended that was a more definite answer than my first. He simply asked, "Okay, how rich?"

I continued to ramble, "Rich, really rich. I mean... the richest man in the world!"

Silence. All of us seemed to have frozen in time after those words.

I realized that I had bungled in making such a premature statement. I had gotten so carried away with my idea of what I wanted to do, that I had blurted out the most stupid thought ever.

"Great, I like that," papa said encouragingly. "There is nothing wrong with becoming the richest man in the world." I was slightly annoyed because I felt papa was teasing me.

"Sorry, papa," I was almost in tears, "I just get frustrated when people ask me what I want to do in life."

My mother put her arms around me and gave me a gentle, reassuring squeeze. Papa tried to lift my spirits as well. "Son, I am serious. There is nothing wrong with dreaming big and aiming to become the richest man in the world. You can be a role model for generations to come. I can help you achieve your dream." Those words had the effect of a soothing balm on my nerves.

"Please tell me more. How did this thought occur to you?" I could tell that he genuinely wanted to know.

I felt grateful. Most parents from middle-class families would condemn their children for wanting to pursue such an ambitious goal, but my parents wanted me to follow my dreams. Their probing questions made me realize that I lacked direction.

I had to address this issue and so, I recalled my interaction with the ashram's trustee, whom everyone called the 'noble businessman'.

I told them that it was he who had said that creating wealth was a blessing and that he could support so many good causes because of the money that he had made.

"But papa, I do not know which line of business I should take up," I admitted dismally.

"Don't worry," he said. "Astrology will show you the way."

That seemed like quite a bizarre reply; I was not sure what papa was getting at. He sensed my confusion and added,

"Astrology, or *jyotish*, is a divine science created by our *Rishis* to guide mankind in tricky situations such as yours."

Until this point in time, I had no idea that my father was interested in astrology.

"Most people do not understand astrology at all, or they have a misconception about the subject and astrologers."

This was not making much headway with me, so I requested that he explain further.

"There is a difference between astrology and the astrologer. Astrology is the science and an astrologer is the scientist. Just because we come across the wrong scientist, who cannot understand the science and its laws, does not mean that the science is imperfect." Yes, that made sense.

"We need to have the right scientist explain the science to us," he stressed. "So, the key is to get the right astrologer who decodes astrology for us."

He was also concerned about the bad reputation that astrology had garnered over the years.

"It is unfortunate that many so-called astrologers have commercialized this field to such an extent that people have lost faith in the science."

I immediately recollected what Chanakya had written in the *Arthashastra*:

*Phonetics, Rituals, Grammar, Etymology, Prosody and Astrology – these are the Vedangas. (1.3.3)*

Oh, yes! Chanakya had studied astrology and astronomy as well and used that knowledge to guide kings through difficult situations.

"Another problem with astrology is that people want to know their future through it. In reality, astrology will only *indicate* the future, but one has to *create* it."

My father was keen on making me understand all the factors that had led to the public disillusionment of this science.

The questioning look on my face was all that he needed to keep talking:

"Okay, look at it this way," papa began, "every person has some innate talent, which we look upon as God's gift to that person. But, instead of focusing on what is our talent and strength, we try to copy others without thinking if we are really made for it." This I understood.

He continued, "A donkey cannot sing. It is not made for it. However, what a donkey can do, other animals cannot, like carrying heavy loads. It is wrong to try and make a donkey sing."

Now, I could draw a parallel between the donkey's example and how we youngsters are forced to take up certain careers, like medicine or engineering, without being naturally inclined towards them.

If everyone identifies what each person is good at, then we can build our future based on that.

"That is where astrology comes into play. It not only shows you what you are good at, but also charts a roadmap for you and helps you reach your destination faster." This helped clear quite a few misconceptions that I had about astrology.

"But remember, you have to walk the path; only following directions or a roadmap will not help," my father smiled at me.

"What about finding a good scientist? How do you go about doing that?" I asked, voicing my scepticism on whether any really good astrologers existed in today's world.

"Yes, there is a friend of mine – a university professor, who has done his PhD in the subject. Let me talk to him and take an appointment for you," papa paused, as he rummaged around for the phone directory.

Chanakya's wisdom from the *Arthashastra* had come to my rescue, to help and guide me in making one of the most critical decisions of my life – choosing a career.

It was only the beginning.

Astrology continued to guide me through every phase of my life, much like a divine light (*jyoti*) from the Lord Himself (*Ishwar*).

Therefore, it was called *Jyot-ish*.

# 28

# The Sanskrit Professor

The astrologer called us to his office. He was a very senior professor in the Sanskrit department of our city's university.

This was only my second interaction with a Sanskrit professor; the first had been my own *Guruji*. Loaded with books in every corner, the Sanskrit department was more active than I had imagined it would be.

As we sat down in the professor's room, he told my father, "Over the years, the demand for learning Sanskrit has increased. All our university courses are full. There is a huge waiting period every year for new students who want to study here."

He had met my father at some Sanskrit language promotion program many years ago, and their friendship had blossomed since. They were both quite fond of each other.

"I created an astrological chart – *Janma Kundali* – for your son," he said, getting down to business.

He had my horoscope in front of him, along with some handwritten notes. I was curious about what he was going to say next.

"It is very unique. I have read many *Kundalis* in my life, but this one is really special. Your boy has very strong willpower. He will do all that it takes to make sure he succeeds in whatever he takes up." I was pleased that someone was praising me in front of my father.

"But the best part is the position of planet Jupiter in his horoscope," he said, referring to his calculations.

I was suddenly intrigued. "What is this about planet Jupiter, sir?"

"In Sanskrit, Jupiter is known as *Guru*, according to Vedic astrology. It signifies luck and fortune. Jupiter rules religion, philosophy, spirituality, wealth and progeny. If favourable, this planet gives name, fame, success, honour, wealth and good relationships."

"Vedic astrology?" I sought more details.

"There are various forms of astrological systems in this world. In India, we follow Vedic astrology, since the foundation of Indian philosophy lies in the *Vedas*." He also cited examples of other systems prevalent in the world.

Then, as if trying to pull my leg, he said, "Even your Chanakya, in the *Arthashastra,* tells the king to study the *Vedas*." Papa had obviously briefed him about my studies.

I tried to recollect where Chanakya had written that and it came easily to me:

*Philosophy, the three Vedas, economics and the science of Politics - these are the sciences (to be learnt by a leader). (1.2.1)*

This was the same chapter in which Chanakya had elaborated on the importance of *Aanvikshiki*.

"In your case, since your *Guru* is powerful, you will make

tremendous progress in whatever path you choose," the professor shot me a wide grin.

For me, '*Guru*' was more a person than a planet. I was visualizing the blessings of a teacher in my life, rather than some planet orbiting in space. It did not matter to me as long as I could succeed in life.

"You can ask me questions and I will guide you," he threw open the floor to me.

"Can I become a successful businessman?" was my first question.

"As I said, your willpower is good. You will succeed in anything that you take up. So, succeeding in business or academics or any other field is not a problem at all." This was comforting to know.

"What kind of business should I do?"

"There are some specific indicators in your chart, which say that fields involving writing, speaking, metals and any other business connected to the colour green would work well for you. In fact, you can even have multiple businesses also if you like; all of them will work well for you."

He paused briefly before continuing, "but you will achieve mental clarity only after sometime. According to the dates, it will take you a few more years until you can start your own business."

That threw me off for a moment. I recovered quickly to voice the most pressing question that now weighed on my mind, "So what should I do now?"

I had completed my graduation and wanted to start some business right away.

"I suggest that, for the time being, you take up a job."

I hated that suggestion.

"This is exactly what I do not want to do. My friends are taking up jobs, but I want to create jobs for others," I told him, hoping he could find an alternative.

"You have no experience of the world at this stage of your life. Work experience in some company will prove very helpful to you. With that experience, you can start your business. Don't take up a job for the salary, take it up for experience," he advised.

When presented like that, it seemed like a good suggestion. I was somehow open to the suggestion.

Looking at my father, he said, "He will also continue his education at every stage of life. He will seek higher education and will love being surrounded by scholars and intellectuals."

That was true. I had earlier thought that being a graduate would be enough for me. It was after my six-month study of the *Arthashastra* that somewhere, the desire for lifelong learning had made its home in my heart and mind.

"Sir, I just saw on the notice board outside that admissions for MA in Sanskrit are open. Can I take admission?"

"I would suggest you start with a basic foundation course in Sanskrit, then you can proceed to do an MA."

Learning the language was an idea that quite appealed to me, but it was later that I learnt that I required a minimum qualification of a bachelor's degree in Sanskrit before I could take up an MA. With no prior academic qualification in the language, I could only take admission to the foundation course.

"You can simultaneously take up a job. It is a weekend course, so you can work during the week and then attend classes on Saturday and Sunday," the professor suggested.

That settled it. The next thing on my agenda was to look for a job.

# 29

# The Interview

I had started on my job hunt. I hated disclosing that to my friends as I had already told them of my intentions to start a business.

One day, as I was reading the papers, I chanced upon an advertisement regarding a vacancy in a large company. The post was that of a business development executive. The word 'business' was what had caught my eye.

I applied and got a call for the interview within a week. This well-known company had started a new line of business and was looking to hire a young workforce to expand its sales and marketing team.

This was the first time I had gone to such a big corporate office. I was dressed in formals and waited along with others in the reception area to be called in for the interview. I noticed that most of them were very anxious.

I struck up an informal chat with the others and realized that some of them needed this job badly. Some came from poor families and this job had the potential to change their fortune forever.

I started telling myself, never belittle a job; it gives dignity to many. It did not matter to me whether I got this job or not, but for thousands, or probably millions, across the globe, it was a make-or-break moment.

My turn was announced. Somewhere in the depths of my being, I did not want to get selected. Not that I had dropped the idea of working, but just the thought that some needy person could benefit more from the opportunity seemed to make more sense to me.

There is a saying: *when you least expect it, you get it.*

During the interview, I could easily answer most of the questions. I had done my research on the company and its products. My confidence level was high and I certainly did not mind if I didn't consequently bag the job.

Then I was asked the most important question by the interviewers: "What is your salary expectation?"

I guess my answer impressed them a lot: "I have applied for the position of a business development executive. How can I ask for a salary if I do not develop the business for the company?"

Within a few minutes, they said, "Okay, you are selected. The training starts next month."

In the time I had before the date I was to join the company, I went to the university and took admission for the weekend Sanskrit foundation course.

A new chapter in my life was about to begin. I was going to work and study simultaneously. I was proud of the fact that I had got my first job in the very first attempt itself.

Some of my peers were still struggling to achieve a breakthrough. I silently prayed for their success, not only because I knew they wanted a job, but also because most of them deserved it and needed a regular income.

I had just one more week left before I was to start working, when I suddenly got a call from the company. "Can you come tomorrow to meet our chairman?" the message was relayed. More than an order, it sounded like a request.

"Of course, sir," was my answer.

I could not figure out what had happened. I thought I had already bagged this job. Was a final round of interview still pending?

This time, I did not take lightly the fact that I was going for another interview. I respected the time they had invested in me and felt a sense of dignity to go again to this corporate giant.

As I entered the reception area, I realized there was no one else in queue for the interview. I had no time to ponder over that; within a moment, I was taken to the chairman's cabin.

I was still trying to figure out what was happening, when I found myself standing before the chairman of one of India's biggest business groups.

For a moment, it felt like a dream. I had seen this man on television, in newspapers and every single place where a business tycoon was invited to speak.

"Come, young man. Have a seat," he motioned to the chair, trying to make me feel comfortable. "Some tea or coffee?"

"No sir, I am fine. A glass of water will do." After ordering the same, he picked up some papers that were lying on his desk.

"I am supposed to address the new recruits on the first day of their training program next month. As a routine practice, I take a look at the final list of selected candidates, so that I know who is joining our team," he said.

"But your CV has impressed me a good deal. That is why I called you here for a discussion," he smiled.

This statement added to my confusion. My CV clearly

showed that I had no work experience. I was a fresher and just a basic graduate. So, what was it that he saw that was so special?

"Sir, what was it in my CV that impressed you?" I asked, figuring I had to say something if I wanted to make sense of what was going on.

"You did this Indology course on Kautilya's *Arthashastra*. This looks amazing. It says you have studied all the 6,000 sutras and your certificate is also attached," he pointed out.

Finally, the fog surrounding this mystery meeting was clearing up. "Sir, that was just a course I did out of interest, not as a professional qualification." It sounded as though I was making out the study of the *Arthashastra* to be a small feat, when, in fact, it was the reason I was sitting in front of one of the biggest business tycoons of the world.

He asked me more about Chanakya, the *Arthashastra* and my understanding of the subject. I told him about *Aanvikshiki* – the science of thinking – and about how leadership should be based on foundations of *Dharma* and everything *Guruji* had taught me.

This discussion, not interview, went on for nearly an hour.

The chairman then said, "I have another offer for you."

"What offer?" I was dazed and confused.

30

# Sharing the Vision

"Apart from your course on the *Arthashastra*, I also saw your interviewer's notes," he showed me my CV with some handwriting scribbled across it.

It read: *He has no salary expectations; wants to develop business first.*

The chairman said, "This is what impressed me the most."

"You know, most of the people who apply for jobs do not come with this kind of mindset. They come here to earn high salaries and for the brand value our company has. For your age, this is a very good attitude.

The reason why I called you here is because I wanted to ask you something," he paused for a moment, as if in deep thought.

"Would you like to work directly under me? In the chairman's office?"

I could not believe my luck! I was getting a dream offer.

"Of course, sir!" I jumped at the opportunity.

"But, but," he cautioned, "it comes with a catch. You will not get any salary at all. In the first offer letter, you have a job and we are paying you a decent salary. However, when you are working under me, you will get no salary at all."

This was definitely another test: he wanted to see if I truly believed in working without an income, or whether it was something I had said merely to impress the company.

He continued, "Remember, your first offer still stands – your job, salary, training and even your travel needs will be provided for, if you choose to be a business development executive. However, if you choose to go with my offer, there is no salary and you will be a small person doing a desk job."

I went over the proposal carefully in my mind. I had just one question:

"Sir, to tell you frankly, I want to be a businessman and the reason I applied for the business development post was so that I can learn from bringing in business. How will I learn about that by sitting in an office?"

"I am a businessman – the entire world knows this. Not many are aware, though, that I am a teacher. I love teaching business," he smiled.

The chairman continued, "That is the reason I keep doing guest lectures at various universities and management institutions. I enjoy sharing my knowledge, but very rarely do I find good students like you. You will have to commit yourself as a student and I will teach you everything about business."

Ah! Another *Guru* for me – and a business *Guru* at that! I recollected a verse from the *Arthashastra*:

*Training and discipline in the sciences are acquired by accepting the authoritativeness of the teachers in the respective sciences. (1.5.6)*

In the section titled *Vriddha-Sanyogah* (Association with Elders), Chanakya teaches us that one learns from experts in various fields.

Here was a golden opportunity for me to learn about business directly from one of the biggest tycoons of the world. I could not thank my stars enough.

"Ready, sir," I promised.

I knew he was already expecting my acceptance. Why else would such an important man waste more than an hour of his time to hold a discussion with me?

"Okay. I will ask my HR team to send you the revised offer letter as a management trainee in the chairman's office," he said, while his secretary took down his instructions.

"But remember, no salary!" Both of us laughed.

My joining date remained the same as that mentioned on the earlier appointment letter. The only difference was that I was supposed to report to the chairman's office first.

I was there before time. I felt privileged. The security guard had been informed that I had direct access to the chairman's office. I sat waiting for my idol to arrive.

When he came, he first noticed me among the others first. "Welcome to your first day in the office." His words signalled to others that I was the man with the big boss.

He asked me to come into his office and be a part of the daily review that he held with his three assistants. They gave him some reports, discussed some meeting schedules and travel itinerary, among others. I was still trying to grasp what were the workings of a chairman's office, when one of his assistants said,

"Sir, the new trainees have arrived. It is time to address them."

He looked at me, "Come, let's go."

As we stepped into the lift, the chairman said, "I like to welcome all the new recruits myself by speaking to them directly on the first day, sharing the vision of our company that has grown in so many years."

When we got out of the lift, we were taken to a room where about 50 new recruits with different profiles were seated. I spotted some of those who had given the same interview as I had.

They were surprised to see me arrive with the chairman instead of being seated among them.

I was particularly glad when I saw the smiling face of another boy, who was hired at the last minute in my place. I remember him telling me how desperately he needed this job.

Each recruit's face bore the same expression as I did on the day I was called to meet the chairman. They were awestruck, being in front of the man who commanded the respect of the entire business world.

He spoke to them for about half an hour about what the company stood for and what was expected of them. Next, he invited questions, which he answered effortlessly, while keeping the tone informal.

It made all of us feel at ease with him and the gigantic organization that we had just become a part of.

He concluded, "I hope that this will be a great learning experience for all of you here and that you will become ambassadors of our company's vision. Remember, we don't just do business, we serve the society through our various businesses."

I was once again asked to join the chairman on the way back to his office.

He looked at me and said, "I have one rule for you, only one."

## 31

# The Chairman's Training

The concept of a 'noble businessman' was now clearer to me. First, the trustee of the ashram and now, my chairman, both wanted to serve society.

"From now on, you will never ask me any questions," was his only instruction. "Whatever you want to understand, you will learn the answers through observation," he said.

I was a little taken aback by this instruction. So, my job was to be a passive follower, just do as I was told and no more?

My chairman then clarified, "When your mind is filled with questions, it is cluttered. Learning needs patience. Once you develop patience, you will find all the answers."

He could see the confusion in my mind. "Don't worry. You will have the freedom to ask questions later. But I will tell you when to ask these questions. For now, keep learning from anything and everything in this company."

His next meeting was scheduled and he asked me to join him.

For many days, I followed him like a shadow. I obeyed his instructions and maintained the role of a silent observer. He took me to meetings and social programs, to his house and to clubs where he was a member, and even to a spiritual organization where he used to study the *Bhagavad Gita* on a weekly basis.

I had joined him to work in his company, but he opened his entire world to me – public and private. Many questions would spring up in my mind, but I resisted asking them.

Later, during some conversation he had with another person, my questions would be answered, directly or indirectly. I knew that he was a great teacher, only his style of teaching was different.

Six months had passed. At one end, I was with my chairman doing nothing, while at the other end, I was attending my Sanskrit classes at the university. I was working very hard to gather knowledge about this great Indian language.

What happened in these six months was a life-changing experience. I do not even know when it happened, but it did. I could feel a great change within me. I was thinking and reflecting more. I deliberated on how this big business group operated at the macro and micro levels. I also used my Sanskrit education to read the *Arthashastra* again. Now, I could understand every new aspect of the words Chanakya had used.

I made notes every day without fail. In one notebook, I wrote what I had learnt in my office each day. Another set of notebooks were devoted to my increasing knowledge of Sanskrit.

By this time, I had over 25 such notebooks. I noted down a verse in the *Arthashastra*, which was an instruction from a teacher to his student:

*During the remaining parts of the day and the night, he should learn new things and familiarize himself with those already learnt, and listen repeatedly to things not learnt. (1.5.15)*

I was constantly learning. I was enjoying every moment. I was not preparing for any exams, but for life's challenges.

One day, the chairman said suddenly, "You can now ask any questions you might have."

This came as a surprise to me, because by this time, my mind had developed the habit of not enquiring about the questions I had in my mind. It took me some time before I could open my mouth to ask a question.

"How does one create wealth?" That is what I had wanted to learn when I first came here.

"Wealth goes through four stages," he began. "The first is wealth identification, the next is wealth creation, followed by wealth management and then wealth distribution," he charted out the path for me.

"If one wants to be wealthy, one has to first identify an opportunity. People usually look for opportunities outside. It should be the other way. Identify your talents and strengths. That is also God-given wealth. Most of us forget to identify this inner wealth."

He continued, "Having found an opportunity does not mean you have become wealthy. One needs to work hard to create wealth. For example, if you know the location of a goldmine, does it mean that you have the gold? One needs to undertake the mining process, refine the gold and finally, what comes out is a result of hard work."

Then he narrated his own experience: "Once, a news reporter asked me about one of our new business ventures. 'Sir, your business has become successful overnight.'

I was surprised by how casually people take wealth creation," the chairman expressed a sense of disgust.

"I replied – yes, we became successful overnight, but the night was very long." Both of us laughed.

"Once we create wealth, we need to manage it well," he continued. "Save it, invest it and keep it for the rainy days. After creating wealth, if we do not manage it well, we will end up back at square one. Do not keep working for money lifelong. Let money work for you." I liked this advice.

Taking a deep breath, he said, "Finally, wealth must be given back to others – this is called wealth distribution."

I wanted to ask a few questions on this. But before I could start, he understood and stopped me, "No more questions now." I became quiet. However, I did not know that there was about to be another cause for surprise.

"Your training in my office is over. From tomorrow onwards, you will be joining our minerals and metals division. Henceforth, you will report to the CEO of the group, not to me."

He picked up the phone and said, "Ask the CEO to come in."

# 32

# My New Boss

The CEO of the minerals and metals division was an experienced man. He was known as a mover in the industry. He was highly qualified and known to be a globetrotter. Any comment from him could impact the stock market trend.

"As I mentioned in the last board meeting, he will join your team from tomorrow," the chairman said to the CEO.

"Sir, I have been getting positive reports about his performance in your office. I will take it from here," were the CEO's first words.

What performance was he talking about? I was just a mute observer. But then, I had been told not to ask any questions, so I let my question and the CEO's positive feedback pass.

"You will meet me once every month. So, even though you will report to our CEO, I will be monitoring your progress," the chairman stated. *My goodness, the chairman has some system of monitoring every person*, I realized.

Then he smiled, "You will be entitled to a salary from tomorrow onwards. He will tell you the details," he said, pointing to the CEO.

"And most importantly, you can ask our CEO any and all

of the questions you want. No restrictions on that." The three of us had a good laugh.

As I left the chairman's office, having been handed over to the CEO, I realized that my mind had been conditioned to not asking any questions. Truly speaking, it did not matter to me at all.

When I returned home that day, I was not even rejoicing at the thought of earning my first salary from next month onwards. Even without being fully aware of it, I had been transformed internally.

The next day, I entered the CEO's office. His cabin was smaller as compared to the chairman's, but it was equally majestic. He, too, carried the sense of authority that the chairman had.

I recollected what Chanakya had stated in the *Arthashastra* – even the minister is a king in his own space.

The minerals and metals division contributed to nearly 40 percent of the group's business. So, in no way could it be considered small. It employed thousands of engineers, technicians and other kinds of employees. It had offices across the country and operations in foreign locations, too.

"Welcome to your new office," were the CEO's first words as I reported for work. "Here is your offer letter. It includes the company policy. I hope the terms and conditions are fine with you," he gave me the paper.

I went through it, as if it really mattered to me. I had been given the designation of Senior Manager – Operations; the salary was four times what would have been my starting salary. I was pleasantly shocked. I knew this company was a good paymaster, but four times was too much for a young boy like me. I signed the paper quietly and took the offer letter.

"Okay. Now, you can ask your questions." It almost seemed like an order.

I finally gathered up the confidence to ask a question, a habit I had forgotten while the boss had been present.

"Sir, I have no technical qualification in this field. Besides this, I came here with the intention of learning business development. How is it that you have given me such a post?"

"Our chairman is a wonderful person. He has the knack of identifying a person's strengths, even if the person himself is not aware of what he or she is," he said.

"When I joined the company years ago, I, too, had no technical qualification. But you will build that along the way. Technical expertise always helps in building a business. And the best way to start is with practical experience on the ground.

That is why we have put you in Operations, so that you can be in touch with the ground realities of our business," he said. "Your job will require extensive travelling. So, please inform your university professors accordingly. Keep them in the loop in case you have to miss some classes," the CEO knew about my weekend Sanskrit course.

The new job was very hectic. I had to go to the mines, which were located in remote areas and even in forests. At times, I had to travel by road for hours to reach a destination. I often felt exhausted and homesick.

From a job that required sitting in the chairman's air-conditioned office to being on the road at all hours with dust all over my body was a sea change for me.

After the initial training to help me understand the business, I was supposed to submit various reports to the CEO from time to time.

I was hardly at home during the holidays. Even when I was

home, I would be attending Sanskrit classes and completing the work pending from the classes I had missed. I had to work very hard, at office and at home.

It had been over a year and I had taken just a week's holiday, that too, only to give my Sanskrit exams at the university. To everyone's surprise, this time, I topped my class.

I went back to the Sanskrit professor. "Sir, now can I take admission for MA in Sanskrit?" He had been observing me closely throughout the year.

"You still require a bachelor's degree in Sanskrit before you can take admission to the master's course. You have a degree in a different field."

He thought a bit and then said, "Alright, apply for the course. Since you have topped the foundation course and you have a certificate in Indology Studies of the *Arthashastra*, I can recommend you as a special case to the Board of Studies. Let's see how it goes from there."

I realized how much the certificate was coming in handy.

I thought of my *Guruji* at this point.

# 33

# Two Bits of Good News

My friends were having a reunion. This time, we had decided to meet in the college where we had studied, rather than meet at a hotel. It had been a long time since I had met them, even though they used to have regular meetings among themselves.

"Where had you disappeared to?" all my friends enquired.

I told them how life had become hectic between work and studies, and how working in the big company was a great learning experience, too.

By this time, I already had two assistants at work. Apart from reporting to a boss, I had also become a boss, asking for reports from others.

All my friends were doing something; they were no longer faced with the question, "What are you going to do in life?" Some had taken up jobs; others had joined their family businesses. One had taken up academics as a career and was pursuing her PhD.

I spent some more time with her to understand how the PhD system works. I had not told anyone about my own desire to do a PhD after completing my MA, a course to which I was eagerly awaiting admission.

"There is a seminar in my college. Would you like to come and present a paper?" Those words reminded me of the only *Arthashastra* conference I had spoken at, after I had come back from the ashram.

"I am not sure if I can speak at a seminar. I have lost touch with research in the last few years. I have been very busy with my work. I don't know if I could really contribute," I shared my apprehension.

"That is not a problem. You can speak on the *Arthashastra* and its application in modern-day business. That will be a good topic. After all, it is a management seminar. You can throw some light on the relevance of ancient wisdom in the modern scenario." I liked my friend's suggestion.

When I got home, my mother smiled as she said, "There was a call for you from the Sanskrit department of the university. They said you could come tomorrow and take admission for the master's course."

I could not believe my ears. The Board of Studies had accepted my request for direct admission to the MA course – a special case indeed. Just then, there was another phone call; it was the CEO. "I need to meet you tomorrow. There is an important message for you from the chairman."

Both pieces of news were welcome.

The next day, I got ready and went to the university to finish my admission process. I went to the Sanskrit professor and thanked him for recommending my case.

He laughed, "I knew it would not be difficult to get your case approved by the board." He was evidently satisfied with the result.

"Remember, however, that the master's course requires a

bigger commitment. You need to attend classes regularly. How will you manage your office time?"

Without thinking twice, I said, "Please don't worry on that front, sir, I will handle that." Thanking him, I rushed to my office, where I was scheduled to meet the chairman.

As my CEO and I entered the chairman's office, I realized that it was not just a routine review of my work and general discussion. There were two other people in the office along with the chairman. They were senior members of the management team. All of them welcomed me with a smile.

The chairman began, "My dear boy, we have good news for you." The good news of getting admission to the MA course had not settled down yet. I wondered what this next piece of good news was.

"The board has decided to promote you to the position of Assistant Director of the Minerals and Metals division of our group."

Oh my god, this was some news!

"You will be the youngest ever in the history of our company to get this senior post in such a short period of time," the CEO added. I had lost the habit of asking the chairman any questions; however, the chairman had developed the habit of answering my unasked questions.

"You have shown tremendous commitment to your work. What you have achieved in such a short period takes decades for others to achieve. You have not only contributed tremendously to the company, but also developed a mindset that a good businessman needs," he said.

"By the way, this is big news for the media. You are going to be famous." The CEO, who was used to facing various television interviews, knew that business journalists would treat this as breaking news.

The energy levels inside the chairman's office were high; everyone was full of praise for my performance. Deep within me, however, there was a sense of sadness. Yet another promotion? I asked myself.

Is this what I had come to this company for? Life was good to me, but was this the life that I wanted to live? A higher post would mean more responsibilities. As I had performed so far, I would keep performing again and again. That would lead to another promotion.

It was a vicious, never-ending cycle.

I had come to the company to learn about business, not to become an employee. In addition, I had just taken admission in a postgraduate course, which required more time commitment for studies.

I had worked like a donkey, and now, the donkey in this company would have to carry a bigger load.

The chairman said, "I have asked the CEO to complete all the formalities. You should get ready for the new role."

We came out of the chairman's cabin. The CEO was overjoyed. "Young man, I am proud of you. You have made it in life. Congratulations!"

Without meeting his eyes, I said in a low tone, "Sir, I would like to offer my resignation."

# 34

# The Connect

The next day, I got up at 4 AM, which was very early for me. I had gotten used to working late nights and not feeling refreshed on waking up in the mornings.

That day was different. I looked at the clock and wondered if I needed to wake up so early. I hit the bed again. However, I soon realized that I did not need any more sleep.

I got up and did my exercises. I had more energy to do the *Surya Namaskar*. After taking a bath, I did my regular *puja* and was ready for the day. I realized I had more time.

I sat down to meditate, and for the first time, I found a deep connect to myself. When I opened my eyes, I saw the rising sun. For a boy accustomed to city life, dawn was not part of the culture. Looking at the rising sun was a divine experience.

As the sun rose, spreading its golden rays, I felt the boy in me had become a man.

"What happened?" Mummy came into my room. She asked, surprised, "Do you have to go somewhere? Why are you up so early?"

Mummy had become used to my erratic travel schedules – taking flights early in the morning, having a car wait outside my house to drive me to another city, coming back late in the night. The only thing she would ask was if food had to be prepared for me.

I knew that and said, "Don't worry, I am not going anywhere. We will have breakfast at the normal time."

I still hadn't given anyone at home, the shocking news that I had decided to quit my dream job. I was waiting for clarity on what I would do next. I knew that I wanted to get into business, though I was still unsure as to what kind of business.

The chairman told me later, "I always knew you would quit our company, but I did not expect it to happen so suddenly." He was concerned about me.

"To promote you was not my decision at all. The CEO recommended it and the board approved the decision. I knew you would be a performer wherever you go. You have proved me right. But I want to help you decide your future course, too."

"Sir, I have learnt a lot here. More than my boss, you have been my mentor. I will require your support throughout my life. At this point, I am not clear what I will do, but that is not my immediate concern. I just want to spend time with myself. I need a break," I said with confidence.

He nodded in understanding. "Go, find your calling in life. I will be happy to help you whenever you need me."

That day, I was preparing for the topic my friend had invited me to present on. I worked very hard on the paper, which was titled 'Management Fundamentals in Kautilya's *Arthashastra*'.

"I am sure it will be path-breaking work," she said when we met up again. I wanted some tips from her on how to refine my research paper. After completing the paper, I submitted it for the seminar, which was now only a few days away.

"Why don't you look at pursuing a PhD degree in the area

of the *Arthashastra*?" she suggested, not knowing in the least that this was what I had already intended to do.

"Doctor," I addressed her. My friend was already half-way into her research. At the end of her research road was a PhD, after which she would be called a 'Doctor', not a medical one, but an academic doctor.

"That is a long way ahead. Don't call me a doctor now."

I liked her reaction and teased her some more. "Doctor ... Madam, start getting used to people addressing this way. It is only a matter of time before it becomes reality," I tried to instill confidence in her. She smiled at having found a friend who understood her deep desire to complete her research and take up an academic career.

My paper presentation in the seminar was well received and highly praised. The head of the department of the management section called me aside and said, "You should work on the philosophy of Kautilya in your research work."

My doctor friend was surprised, "Do you know, he is the head of the department and is known for his critical opinions. If he has appreciated you, it means you are very good. Congratulations!"

"Of course! I am good at everything I do," I said with attitude.

"Ah, you and your inflated ego," she said, looking away.

We had a hearty laugh. I was happy that I was finding my place back in the research world. "Thank you, Doctor," I said, looking into her eyes. I could feel a connection. There was complete silence between us, as if time had come to a halt.

"Will you marry me?" I asked.

The silence between us continued...

# 35

# The Way Ahead

Doctor and I had graduated from the same college. We were not in the same class, but had common friends. Never in the past had I imagined that she would be the girl I would want to marry.

After I proposed to her, I was surprised at myself. It happened so suddenly that I had not thought of the consequences. The bigger surprise was that she accepted my proposal immediately.

They say that when you are in love with someone, never miss the opportunity to say it. However, when she accepted the proposal to be my life partner, I suddenly realized that I was at a stage of life where I had no direction. Why, then, was I asking for a higher responsibility in life, like marriage?

I felt guilty and went back to her, "I love you, but you are always free to change your mind and choose another person." I wanted her to reconsider her decision.

"What is the matter? Do you have another girl in mind?"

"No, you are the only person I have ever proposed to in my life, but I don't want our relationship to fail." I was nervous. "I do have no direction in life. People consider me a fool for leaving such a great job in that big company. Anyone else in my place would have gotten married after holding such a dream job, but I don't even know what to do next," I explained.

She touched my shoulder and said, "Don't worry. I know you will make it big one day. I did not like you because of what you have, but because you have the potential to do something… something really big."

"You know, I have a dream – a silly dream in life," I wanted to share, "to become the richest man in the world… " I was waiting for her to laugh at me.

Instead, she said after a pause, "We are already rich; we have each other. It is only a matter of time before we have money." Usually, Indian women face a lot of social pressure to get married. In her case, she could wait until she completed her PhD. And so, I had some time to decide about my next step in life.

During that time, I got a chance to visit the Kumbh Mela, a majestic gathering of humanity at one place. The atmosphere was divine. I had gone with my friends to take a holy dip in mother Ganga.

As we were walking along the shore of the river, I saw a group of foreigners walking next to us. They had a travel guide, who spoke about the surroundings as they photographed the whole of Kumbh Mela.

After the walk, we refreshed ourselves over tea at a small teashop, when this group of foreigners joined us. We exchanged greetings and started a conversation.

"Where else can we travel in India? We have all the information with us, but do you know of a place where we can really feel India and capture the experience on camera to take back home with us?" One of them asked us.

"You can never truly capture India on camera," I said almost sarcastically.

"India is not just a place to see or a place you just travel through. You will have to understand India from a different outlook. It has an energy level that can change you. Try to feel that energy level wherever you go; that is the spiritual side of India." The foreigners were amazed by my answer.

"India has the Taj Mahal as well as the Ajanta and the Ellora caves, but it also has a history and philosophy to offer. It has various foods and festivals, but it also has a culture which is spiritual," I continued to explain my pride in my country.

"Are you a tour guide or travel agent?" asked one of the tourists.

"Not at all," I smiled. However, as we walked back to the camp where we were staying on the banks of the Ganga, I was deep in thought.

I thought about the number of tourists who came to India and the demand for capable tour guides who could tell them interesting stories about our history and culture. The setting sun's rays fell on my eyes. I looked up and suddenly visualized the demand for and supply of tour guides.

I called up Doctor, who had not come with us. "Listen, I have my answer," I said in excitement over the phone.

"What answer?" she was trying to understand.

"I mean the question I have been struggling with... which line of business I want to get into. I want to be in the travel business." There was a sense of fulfillment in me when I said this.

On the other side, there was complete silence.

"Let me explain this to you when I come back." I did not want to say more than that.

That night, when all my friends had gone to sleep, I took

a walk on the bank of the Ganga. I was alone, but I was not feeling lonely. I was feeling full of life.

I knew that mother Ganga had inspired millions of people to find their inner calling. Ganga is not just another river; legend has it that it was brought down to the earth from the heavens by the penance of a great *Rishi*. For generations, the river has been flowing, purifying all the people who come to her.

In the Kumbh Mela, in the divine presence of mother Ganga and in an informal discussion with a group of foreigners, I had found my way ahead.

# 36

# The Business Plan

I did some research on the tourism industry – the worldwide trends and how the industry operated. In the case of some countries, I found that their entire economies depended on tourism.

People travel for various reasons, such as for adventure, education, business or relaxation. India had multiple reasons for travelers to come here.

We had a small share of inbound tourists, those coming into India. The potential was huge.

I put the entire business opportunity on paper and explained it to my Doctor. "It's huge, very huge," I said. "There are many travel agents in India today, but no really good tour guides or tour operators. We can develop this sector in a big way."

"What about the investment in this business?" she asked dispassionately.

"That's the best part. We do not require any investment in the first stage of business." She was confused. How can you start a business without any investment?

"The best part of the travel business is that the customer pays first and the service is offered later," I said.

She was still confused. "Let me explain; when you travel by train or plane, you always pay first, right?" She nodded her head in agreement.

"So, you pay in advance and use the services later." She was beginning to understand.

"Now, what happens if you book a plane ticket and you cancel it at the last moment and do not travel?"

"I get a refund after some cancellation charges," she said.

"That is the point. If you travel, you pay in advance, allowing the company to use your money even before you use their services. If you do not travel, you still pay a small amount in the form of cancellation charges. So, either way, the company is making a profit on day one itself."

My description of the travel business continued. "Now extend this reasoning to a tour package. As a travel agent, you offer a full tour, inclusive of food, travel and accommodation. You include all the services in your offering. You sell that and you are into big business."

"Great, sounds promising," she added.

"With this kind of advance money, we can start the business in a small way. It is only when we need to scale up the business ladder that we will require an investor." Both of us were pushing each other to develop this idea further.

It seemed so easy. I realized only later that many things looked easy on paper, but in reality, there were many practical challenges. However, the good news was I knew where I had to focus – the travel business.

I announced to my parents that I would be starting a travel business. They were encouraging as usual.

"Can I tell my parents, too?" Doctor asked.

I realized that she was waiting for the right moment to break the news of our relationship to her parents. Now that I was on the way to start my business, she would have an answer to the difficult question a girl's father would ask, "What does the boy do?"

"Let's wait for some time, until the business starts doing well," I suggested.

She was not too happy with the answer, but what else could a young girl of marriageable age do, when she had to maintain a balance between her parents and the love of her life?

"You said that you would wait until you complete your PhD," I reminded her.

"Yes, but my parents have a different view. They say that my PhD studies can continue after marriage, too." She explained that numerous proposals had been coming her way and her parents were seriously considering some of them.

I was completely enthusiastic about my business idea, and here was a very good reason to make me feel like an unsuccessful person again.

Women are gifted psychologists. They can read your face and understand what you are thinking. She came closer and said, "Don't worry about that. I will handle my parents. Now get on with your business, and let us make it big."

"Let us make it big... " Those words from my Doctor encouraged me. I loved to think big, but the other word was more soothing for me – let *us* make it big. She was now a part of my dream, my business.

I called up my *Guruji*, as well as the trustee at the ashram, where I had studied the *Arthashastra*, to take their blessings. To the trustee and the noble businessman, I said, "Sir, you inspired me to get into business. Let me become like you."

He replied, "You will become better than me." That made me feel good.

After a pause, he asked, "Do you know why?"

I waited for him to answer the question himself. "Because you have studied the *Arthashastra* at a very young age before getting into business. I was not that privileged."

The next call went to my *Guruji*. "Remember to study a few verses of the *Arthashastra* every day. It will show you how to tackle day-to-day problems the Chanakya way."

My destiny was about to change.

# The First Step

With some apprehension, I called up the chairman of the company where I had worked. I was not sure whether he would appreciate an employee, to whom he had offered an excellent opportunity, calling up to ask for his blessings.

"Come over," he said, "I have been wondering where you had disappeared to." His words were very encouraging.

Meeting the chairman once again was a privilege. I explained my idea and business plan to him. He listened with interest. "Travel is a good line of business. I always wanted to get into it, but never had the time to consider it seriously."

When the Chairman said these words, I felt happy that such a successful businessman had endorsed me. However, his next few words were even better, "Maybe I will fulfill that dream through you."

So, it seemed I had found an investor for my business, but this was not the right time to ask for money. I wanted to prove myself first. I wanted to think big, but start small.

The first step I took was to organize a one-day spiritual tour to some of the famous temples in the city that I lived in. I expected a small number of people to enroll for this temple tour.

I had organized everything myself – studied the history of the temples, made arrangements for food, booked the bus and taken care of all the other things that go into making a day tour.

As the chairman had taught me, knowing the basics of any business helps to scale up the business. It was an important factor. It was almost like organizing a picnic. I enjoyed it.

Interestingly, most of the people who came for the trip were known to me. One of the surprise guests in the tour was my prospective mother-in-law. My Doctor had marketed the trip to her family.

"It is one of my college friends, someone you know. He is starting a travel business. It is a one-day trip to temples around our city. Mamma, why don't you go?"

This was her pitch to her mother, so that she could see her prospective son-in-law in action.

Doctor herself did not come, even though I wanted my life partner to be a part of my first step in business. She probably wanted her mother to judge me independently. My mother, too, had joined the trip to see her son's first performance. She paid for her expenses in the trip, in spite of my resistance to take money from her.

The best part was that my mother and to-be mother-in-law were seated next to each other in the bus throughout the day. They were meeting each other for the first time. Ladies do not require introductions or a reason to start talking.

I am sure by the end of the day they knew everything about each other – family, native place, food habits, various interests and what not. What a way to start a marriage alliance!

I played the role of a good tour guide, tour manager and host. Most of the travelers were senior citizens. I had to take special care of them while getting into and off the bus.

There was a small hitch during the trip – a flat tyre. However, it was replaced immediately, and for me, it was a great lesson to have a good backup plan during every future trip.

By the end of the day trip, I had received praise from everyone, but I was seeking blessings from everyone. Both my mother and Doctor's mother even exchanged phone numbers, so they could stay in touch with each other. I only smiled at the way my Doctor's plan had worked.

I was exhausted and wanted to hit the bed. Just then, the phone rang. I knew it was my Doctor calling, "How was the trip?" She asked as if she did not know!

My mother had recounted every detail of what happened during the day to my father while serving us dinner. I am sure the same story would have been repeated at the Doctor's house.

I said to my Doctor on the phone, "If you do not know what happened during the day, go ask your mother."

These words made her feel shy. "Now, go and tell your parents you want to marry me," I ordered.

This time, it was her turn to resist. "No, not now, let the right time come," she said in a low tone.

I finalized the accounts of the trip that day itself and realized that I had made a small profit. I took that amount to my parents, and placing it in front of them, I said, "This is due to your blessings. Thank you."

Both my parents gave me a hug. This small beginning was important for me and for them as well. I also realized that though my aim was to induce more foreign travelers to come to our country, there was a huge demand from domestic travelers as well.

India was changing. Indians also aspired towards world-class travel experiences and did not mind paying extra for great service.

As I was thinking on how to manage the next trip better, I fell asleep.

# 38

# Vendors to Partners

The next morning, I got up and started to study a few pages of the *Arthashastra*. The first sutra that I came across was directly relevant to me.

> *Rulership can be successfully carried out (only) with the help of associates. One wheel alone does not turn. Therefore, he should appoint ministers and listen to their opinion. (1.7.9)*

I realized that I had started my first business, but it was a one-man show. If I had to scale up the business, I needed more associates.

The travel business was dependent on many vendors and suppliers. They were the people who owned buses, the hotels where we stayed, the airlines and the railways which gave us the logistics to take people from one place to another. To organize a tour properly required tremendous coordination among all these people.

My first decision was to call them not my vendors or suppliers, but partners. Only when we become partners would we take ownership of what we do and strive towards excellent service standards.

The next step was to build a strong network of companies that would become my partners – tour agents, tour guides, hotels, industry associations and so on.

I made a list of the various groups that were part of the tourism industry and realized that the industry was huge. There were so many players in this big game. From multinational corporations to small companies with a few people working as travel agents, it provided employment to so many people.

I also found so-called travel agents, whose only service was to book cars on the phone. Some ran their businesses from home, while others did so from big, air-conditioned offices.

When I went around meeting these people and learning all I could about this industry, there were mixed reactions from those I met. Some big companies ignored me; they considered me a new entrant who did not know anything. Some small-timers met me with a lot of enthusiasm, hoping that I would give them good business.

Then, I met a 70-plus man who shared his experience, "The best way to learn fast is not to meet everyone individually, but to go to a travel fair or exhibition, where most of the industry comes for exchange of business." He also told me that the next big exhibition was just a month away.

I had to pay a nominal fee to enter this big exhibition, but I was happy that the return on investment was very high. Stall after stall gave me good exposure to various tour products and services on offer.

During the three-day exhibition, I collected brochures and leaflets from all of the stalls. I also attended the afternoon lectures and sessions taken by industry experts and diligently made notes. I made many friends and realized that all of these were my future partners in business. It was truly a win-win situation for all of us. Tourism was an interdependent industry, and we all needed each other.

I would give them clients, and they would in return, provide their best services, such as good hotels for accommodation or good vehicles for travel. The client on the other end was a tourist, who wanted to explore new places at the most reasonable cost without compromising on quality.

It was the last day. People were packing up their stalls and the organizers were happy to have successfully organized yet another exhibition. Before leaving for home, I went to the food stall for a sandwich and coffee. A mature-looking person was sitting next to me and he struck a conversation with me. I wanted to know what attracted him to this travel exhibition.

"I came to India on a visit and wanted to check out the new developments that India had to offer as a tourism destination," he explained.

He was a person of Indian origin, based abroad for three generations. He was the president of an Indian association there, which had organized various activities in that country. The events included celebration of festivals, such as Diwali, Holi or Navaratri. They also hosted Indian politicians who came to their country and showed the strength of Indians settled there.

"A few years ago, our Indian association organized a tour to Haridwar. Everyone was extremely happy with it," he said. "We were thinking of another trip to India as a group, so I came here to look for places." This was the purpose of his visit.

"What kind of places do you want to go to?" I enquired.

"Hmm…I am not really sure. We do not want the standard Taj Mahal and Jaipur trips, because most of us have seen those places. We are looking at something that will touch our souls."

He continued, "Last year, a *Sadhu* from India came to our

country and gave a spiritual discourse on the *Ramayana*. We were thrilled to see the beauty of the *Ramayana* and all of us back home want to visit these places."

"Which places?" I was beginning to see an opportunity.

"Ayodhya – where Ram was born, Panchavati – where Ram, Lakshman and Sita spent their exile, Rameshwaram... all the places mentioned in the *Ramayana*," he answered.

"So you mean a *Ramayana* circuit?" I wanted to confirm.

"Yes, a *Ramayana* tour customized for us," he said excitedly.

"How many people can be expected if one organizes it?" I checked with him.

"About 200 or so, but lots more may want to come."

"Can I organize it for you?" I saw a business opportunity and seized it.

"You, can you do it?" he was happy, yet not sure a young boy like me could deliver. After a little more thought, he said, "Ok, send me the details."

That was just the beginning of the biggest breakthrough for my business.

# 39

# The Big Trip

I was a small startup businessman with no marketing budgets. Usually, people spend lots of money to get clients, but I had no such financial support.

If I could turn work around my client's requirement, something magical might happen. I opened the *Arthashastra* and got another tip:

> *Be ever active in the management of the economy because the root of wealth is economic activity; inactivity brings material distress. Without an active policy, both current prosperity and future gains are destroyed. (1.19.35, 36)*

Chanakya had stressed upon activity to create wealth. I could have easily written off the business opportunity, saying I had no previous experience. However, if I worked towards my goal actively, I could create prosperity.

I did some research and spoke to some experienced travel agents, whom I had met during the exhibition. I made a blueprint of the '*Ramayana* Circuit' and asked them about the travel arrangements, accommodation and other requirements any first-time tourist may have.

"How many tourists will you have?" This was everyone's standard question.

I had to act smart and said, "Two hundred to begin with, but if you give me a good deal, the number may be higher." To all the people I spoke to, it looked like a very good number. They started taking me more seriously during the discussion.

In a week's time, I had prepared a travel plan with all the details – the day-wise itinerary, types of accommodation, choices of food and everything else that the tourists wanted. I then called up the person I had met during the exhibition.

"I was thinking of you and our discussion," he was happy to hear from me.

"Sir, I have a rough plan ready for the trip that you wanted," I said with pride.

"Good. Send it across to me. I am leaving India tomorrow. I had some discussions with my association members and all of them seemed to be excited about the idea of a spiritual tour to India," he explained.

It was good news for me that the trip was equally serious for them as for me.

With a laugh, he said, "I hope you have put the right price for us."

I knew that all decisions in business are based on economics. However, before I could say anything, he continued, "Don't worry on that front; we are quality-conscious. If you deliver, we will pay you better than what you have quoted, and also give you more business in the future." He ended the conversation.

For two weeks, the trip was discussed in detail among the gentleman, the Indian association abroad and myself. They liked my proposal and tour plan, and I started adding more inputs as per their requirements – food should be vegetarian; there should not be more than two people in one room; buses should be air-conditioned; the trip should not be too hectic. There were many things for me to learn as well.

Finally, he called one day and said, "We are going ahead with the trip set up by you, young boy. Let us know how to send the advance money." I was thrilled. I did not know how to respond. I was myself on a journey to make it big in the travel industry. Keeping my excitement in check, I asked, "Sir, how many people will be coming?" This was to make sure that I got the numbers right.

"Well, we had planned for about 200 people, but the demand is higher. We might have about 300 people. I am resisting increasing the number beyond that. If I let go, there may be 500 people."

Demand for 500 people? I did not want to appear greedy, and continued listening to his side of the story.

"You know, young man, taking on so many people is a major responsibility. After all, if anything goes wrong, I will be blamed," he said in a serious tone.

"I understand, sir." After a pause, I said, "I take full responsibility for the entire trip. Please rest assured that every requirement will be handled with personal care."

Like a grandfather, he asked me, "Young man, can I ask you something?"

"Please do, sir," I was listening.

"I checked your background and found that you have no experience in handling such big tourists groups coming from abroad. Then, how are you so confident about making this tour a success?"

I was surprised that he had done research on me. I did not want to lie to a man who was taking such a big risk on me.

I said honestly, "Sir, it is a *Ramayana* trip. The first thing I did before planning the trip was to pray to Lord Rama himself."

I paused. "I come from a spiritual family. My parents and grandparents have taught me that work should be done with devotion. For me, this is not just another tour; it is a service to the devotees of Lord Rama. He will give me the strength to do it, the way he gave strength to Hanuman to do his duties," I explained.

I do not know how these words came into my mind at that moment, but I meant them with all my heart. I wanted to be a devotee in this trip, rather than a businessman.

Finally, when the group arrived after a couple of months, it comprised 650 tourists! The demand was so high, it was apparent that the gentleman had confidence in me.

The 20-day trip across India was a lot of hard work. At the end of the trip, however, every person was not just happy but spiritually elevated. An old lady in the group blessed me, "May you become like Hanuman to Lord Rama!" The gentleman who had given me this opportunity said, "We are very happy. We are going to give you a big tip."

He smiled, "Start working out a *Mahabharata* tour."

# 40

# The Spiritual Co-traveller

My tours took off and there was no looking back. From the *Ramayana* trip to *Mahabharata* tours, I started designing such unique trips that people from abroad kept pouring in. I was reading the *Arthashastra* and more guidance came from Chanakya:

> *In work that can be achieved with the help of an associate, he should resort to a dual policy. (7.1.18)*

I thought about the deeper meaning of this sutra. I realized that working with a partner is better than doing all the work yourself. In such a partnership, one should think of a dual policy, meaning a win-win situation.

I had partners in the form of vendors and suppliers in the tourism industry, but I required a business partner. I already had my hands full and could not stretch myself much more. I had some junior employees, but they required my guidance. I decided I needed to get a good partner, so that my business could grow to the next level.

As I was thinking about all of this, Doctor called up, "My PhD thesis is in the last stage of submission." I could not figure out whether she was happy or sad about that. For a person who was working towards her PhD, it was like coming to the end of the journey. Then why did she not sound happy?

"I can't stretch it any more. We need to tell our parents," she said in an assertive voice.

When we met up in the evening, I realized that Doctor had been trying her best to resist all discussions of marriage at home, using the excuse of her PhD studies. Now, even that was not a valid excuse.

"Will you tell your parents or shall I tell mine first?" She had been waiting for this moment.

I paused for a moment. I had been struggling with my business for quite some time. I had done well, but had not made enough money yet.

All that I earned was being invested back into the business. The struggling phase was not over yet, but the good times were slowly arriving.

I needed a business partner, but I realized that first, I required a life partner. I had the confidence that I could do anything in life, so I was ready.

I went to my parents and told them about this Doctor in my life. Both of them knew her as my friend from college, but did not know that we felt for each other this way.

During the discussion, I realized that my mother had been wondering about the blossoming friendship between Doctor and me. At the same time, my mother and Doctor's mother had also become good friends, ever since they met during my first organized trip.

In the other family too, the news was taken quite positively. They knew me, and because her father was a businessman himself, he did not mind the struggling phase of my career. The families met and an engagement date was decided. For most of our friends, it came as a pleasant surprise, and everyone was happy.

The best love marriage is the one that is arranged by parents. Even though we came from different communities, the mindset of both families matched. Both sides of the family were very involved in the engagement ceremony. The engagement was a semi-grand event. We were going to be united for life.

While deciding an auspicious date for the marriage, Doctor had only one request. "Let us get married after six months. I will get my PhD degree by then." She was in the last stages of reaching her aim of receiving a doctoral degree and did not want marriage to be a distraction. None of us had any problems in agreeing to this.

My father took me aside and I was fascinated by his beautiful perspective on marriages in India. "In India, we do not consider marriage as just another relationship. It is not just between you and your spouse, or just between your family and her family. It is a relationship between both of you and God.

When the father gives the bridegroom his daughter's hand, he gives him a spiritual companion for life. Both of you have to walk the spiritual path together." I was moved by the way marriage was weaved into divinity.

"Do you know that in Sanskrit, a wife is known as *Sahadharmacharini*?" he asked.

"*Saha-dharma-charini*, meaning a spiritual co-traveler." He referred to a shloka in the *Ramayana* and said, "Every human being is on a spiritual journey to discover God. Your husband or wife should be a supporter on that journey, not a distraction.

If such spiritual foundations are laid down in a marriage, the relationship becomes stronger and more profound. Every marriage will go through ups and downs, facing challenges unique to them. Having a spiritual base helps the couple to stand together and finally make the home a temple to live in." When I told Doctor about this, she too was moved.

A few months after the engagement, she got her doctoral degree. Now, the whole world would officially call her a doctor.

Our marriage was the most beautiful event of our lives. Both families were bound to each other in love. My marriage was attended by every single person who was important to me – my *Guruji*, *Guruma*, the trustee and noble businessman, the big businessman, the CEO under whom I had worked, apart from our numerous common friends.

A new chapter in my life had begun. I had been promoted to the position of husband.

# 41

# The Next Stage of Growth

B eing in the travel business had its advantages. I saw one of the biggest advantages when I was organizing my honeymoon.

A travel agent with whom I had tied up for my own business had become a good friend of mine. He was a specialist in honeymoon packages and knew some exotic places. Believe it or not, he sponsored my whole honeymoon trip!

"Don't worry about the cost. It is all in the family," he said. He made sure that the hotels we stayed in and the vehicles we used were of the best quality, and we did not have to pay for any of this. We had the time of our lives.

Doctor had only one complaint, "How can a husband not spend money on his own honeymoon?" There was a certain joy in seeing a man spend on his wife.

She suggested an alternative, "You will take me for a honeymoon every year." I was stunned. "Also, make sure it is a new place every time," she demanded.

How could I say no to the first demand of my love? This was a deal for life. Every year since the promise was made, we have been going to different places to celebrate our wedding anniversary. Both of us look forward to this annual outing.

Back home, I had realized that I required new strategies to expand my business. I had to recruit new staff, spend more on marketing, explore new markets and move to a bigger office. My business was doing well, but the money was not enough to take the next giant leap.

As a practice, I looked into the *Arthashastra* for guidance:

*If situated between two stronger kings, he should seek shelter with one capable of protecting him. (7.2.13)*

"Who is the stronger king who would protect me?" I thought. I could think of only one person... my big businessman, the chairman of the company where I had previously worked.

I also recollected what he had said to me upon my resignation. He had said, "Go, find your calling in life. I will be happy to help whenever you need me."

I really required help from him to scale up my business. So, I took an appointment and went to meet him.

"You are on the right track. You need to make a good business plan," he suggested.

"Any business that wants to grow should be scalable and should have a good management team." I had come to ask for funds, but I realized I had not carefully thought over the various aspects that he was indicating.

"You need to hire professionals from the industry. They will come with experience, which is important. One cannot grow a business with just one brain. We require many brains along with good hands," this was his experience talking.

"Let me do some thinking myself and next week, we will

make the business plan together." I was only listening, rather than asking.

For the first time since beginning my business venture, I was worried. I knew I had to scale up, but I did not think I required people with industry experience to handle my company henceforth.

When I met the chairman the next week, he had a group of people with him who made up a part of his strategy team. They made a detailed presentation about industry dynamics, government policies and the market potential of the tourism industry.

The chairman continued, "You see, there is big business potential here, but we need to be a game changer. We should not just follow the traditional path, but make a new one that other players will follow."

After some thought, he said, "Let us put this business into automation mode. For that, we need to use the best available technology. That is the way to proceed." The others made a note and a new budget for IT was added to the business plan.

"The world is our market, and we have to capture it through computers." Those were the days when computers were being introduced into the business not just as calculators, but as strategy drivers.

"We will be the first travel company in India to scale up in this manner," the chairman said excitedly.

During the next couple of meetings, the chairman's finance team was involved in working out the monetary details. They reached a big number in terms of the money that needed to be invested in the business.

This amount was much higher than what I had initially thought of asking him in my limited judgement on the matter.

The chairman then asked me a difficult question, "How do you want the shareholding pattern to be?"

I was not prepared for such a discussion. I realized only later that when an investor contributes to your business, he also receives a stake in your company, because he automatically becomes a shareholder.

Why should I give a major share of the business that I have created to someone else? I thought. I realized that the chairman would not just be investing money; I would also be required to share all the details of my business with him. I was fearful of losing my freedom as an entrepreneur.

Would I once again become an employee and report to him on a daily basis? Is this what I had left a job for... to come back to square one? I was now reluctant to take any money from him. He was asking for shares today; he may want to take over my business tomorrow.

"Forget it. I am fine as a small businessman," I had almost concluded, when...

# 42

# Guidance from a Childhood Friend

I was facing a unique challenge. I wanted more investment for growth; at the same time, I was not prepared to give up control of the business I had built from scratch.

Chanakya always suggested the help of friends in difficult circumstances. I had a good friend, a childhood friend who was my sounding board in all difficult matters. I met him and explained my situation.

This childhood friend was working in a big multinational company as the head of finance. He, too, had grown very fast in his career. He was exceptionally good in giving strategic advice and guidance in business.

He said, "Every businessman who wants to grow with the help of investors faces this situation. You need to grow, but you are not ready to let go."

"He is asking for shares in the company," I reiterated.

"What else will he ask for?" he questioned me. I did not have a clear answer.

He explained, "Anyone who invests his money is entitled to his rightful share of the business. For you, it is business; for him too, it is business. So, it is fair that you discuss the shareholding pattern in detail."

"Look at the bright side," he added, "you not only get the money, but you also receive from him the rich experience of running such a big company. You are lucky in a way."

I was not convinced at all. My friend could read my mind and went on to explain with an example.

"For every mother, her child is important. The mother is attached to the child, and gives it all the love and care required. She feeds the child, takes care of it in sickness, teaches it to walk and talk." I could see that as a businessman, my company had been nurtured as a child from day one.

"Then comes the most important challenge – admitting the child to a school. It is most difficult to let the child go to an institution that was previously unknown to both the mother and the child. The child will also resist meeting strangers.

However, the mother also knows that school education is required for preparing the child to face the challenges of the world...

Do you know who the most important person in school is?"

I was quick to respond, "The teacher... "

Smiling, he said, "Exactly. Even though the mother is the child's first teacher, there is a limitation to what she can impart to him. The mother knows that the child has to go to school and learn from specialized teachers." I got his point now.

He explained further, "In the case of a business investor too, one should not just look at the amount of money the investor gives you, but also whether that investor will be your teacher." This chairman was the best business teacher I had ever met.

"You are lucky, my friend. You are not only getting an investor, but also one of the finest and most respected businessmen in our country as your partner." My friend was very happy for me.

As a final word of advice, he said, "Don't think twice. It is a golden opportunity to grow your business. Grab this opportunity with both your hands."

"You know we have been childhood friends, but over the last few years, my respect for you has only grown," he added.

"Respect?" I wanted to clarify.

"Yes, respect. While most of us work in big companies with fat salaries, we cannot take the risk of becoming an entrepreneur like you. Like me, you too, had a choice to work with this chairman at a senior position with a fat salary. But you decided not to take it," he became slightly emotional.

"Now, the same person wants to be your partner, wants to invest in your business. What more could you ask for?"

As we parted, he looked into my eyes and said, "You are not just my friend, but my role model. One day, I too, want to quit this big job and start my own small business."

I gave him a pat on the back and said, "Really? You will be a better businessman than me. Look at me, even though I am running my own business, you are advising me on how to get ahead."

He laughed, "It is easier to give advice than to follow it yourself."

I was happy to have found another direction in life. I accepted the chairman's offer and we structured the shareholding pattern. "Let us plan a big launch," he suggested, "that we have arrived on the world platform. Version two of your company... "

I stopped him, "Sir, our company." He laughed.

I realized that with the chairman coming in as an investor and partner, many things about my business had changed. My confidence level shot up. I was surrounded by professionals and experts from across the globe.

We planned the launch venue to be a five-star hotel. The chairman and his team took over the launch of my company's new avatar. There was great media presence.

Some of the biggest industry giants came for the event. The chairman himself introduced me to everyone with pride. I was also interviewed by many TV channels.

My childhood friend, who was part of the event said, "Imagine if you had denied the offer, would you see such a grand leap for your company?"

I nodded and said, "The mother will always be happy to see the child grow under the guidance of the teacher." We hugged each other.

# 43

# Doctor's Request

Doctor had easily adjusted to her new home – her husband's home. She got along very well with my parents and relatives. For me, this was a good sign.

In India, marriages are different. I was invited by various friends and relatives for lunch or dinner at their homes.

I thought these invitations would taper off after a short period, but they continued for over a year. I was managing between work and the role of a husband.

I also understood how daughters think in our culture. The daughter leaves the parents, who nurtured her and gave her all the love, care and education, to begin her new role as a wife and daughter-in-law. She accepts the new family as her own, but she can never leave her parents' family. Until death, she has to take care of both the families.

After completing her PhD, Doctor started to teach at the university. Being an expert in her field, she was travelling quite frequently for seminars and conferences.

Over dinner one evening, she suddenly asked, "When are you planning to do your PhD?"

The question took me by surprise. In the process of building my business, I had let go of my dream of pursuing a doctoral degree. This question suddenly woke me up to my past. "PhD? No, not for me... "

Even before she could ask, I gave my explanation. "I am building a business; I have lots of commitments. How will I be able to go through the entire academic process again? I don't think that will be possible... I have lost my passion for studying."

Doctor was smart; she did not push me any further. She had a different strategy in mind.

"Are you free this Saturday? Can you come to the university? My students were asking about you. If you can, they would like to spend some time with you and hear about your experience of growing a business."

"Your students have been asking about me?" I did not understand.

"They saw your interview on TV the other day and are aware of what you are doing. They were asking if you could come there to deliver a lecture on your business model." I was curious. I did not know that people were tracking me.

Both my parents joined the discussion. Mother said, "Even my friends saw the interview on TV and complimented me." Father added, "Some even saw your photo with the chairman in the newspaper."

My ego had become bigger. I felt happy to know that many people knew of my achievements as a businessman. "But I do not have time to prepare for any lecture," I told Doctor.

"It will not be a formal lecture, just an informal interaction with the students," she wanted me to feel like it was no big deal.

As I was thinking it over, she said, "Come for just an hour. Talk about how the business started, how you ran the business and how the big investor came in – all the experiences of changing your mindset from an employee to an entrepreneur."

Father added, "You can also describe how the *Arthashastra* has helped you at every stage of your business. The Chanakya-connect will also inspire the young boys and girls to study our ancient Indian wisdom."

Doctor continued, "My students will be happy to listen to your real-life experiences. They may have a few questions which you can address towards the end."

I felt at ease now. I did not have to prepare a research paper; just tell stories, my stories. "Okay. At what time should I come on Saturday?"

"Let me confirm tomorrow after I go to the university." The next evening, Doctor said, "Is 10.30 AM on Saturday fine with you?" I said that it was.

Doctor was excited, "You know, when I said that you were coming, the message spread like wildfire among the students and faculty. Now, there is a demand for students from other groups to be added, too. The best part is that even the teachers want to listen to you, including the head of my department."

I felt nervous and worried now. "You said it would be an informal discussion; this is turning out to be much more than that. What will I speak about?"

"The same stories that you would have told my class. The only difference is the audience will be bigger. How does that matter?"

My mother joined in. "Can I come, too? This way, I will be able to see the place where my daughter-in-law teaches and listen to my son in front of an audience."

Doctor was more than happy, "Great idea, Mom! You will be able to meet my colleagues. They always appreciate the food you send for me." These ladies have a way of getting things done.

The daughter-in-law then looked at her father-in-law said, "Papa, you too join, please."

Looking at my father's face, I realized that he was just waiting to be invited.

I interrupted, "That is fine, but now, don't go and invite your parents." Doctor's face fell. "Okay, I'll call them next time."

I was nervous, but deeply happy inside. I was going back to an educational institution, to a place where I loved to be. I felt as if I was reconnecting with myself.

And then, Saturday arrived...

# 44

# The Lecture of an Indian Businessman

Doctor asked me to wear a formal suit, and when I did so, she said I looked quite charming. That boosted my confidence as all of us made our way to the university.

I realized that what had started as a small idea had become a big seminar. My session was organized in the auditorium and over 200 students were supposed to attend, along with professors of different departments.

I was first taken to the senior-most professor and the head of the department where my wife used to teach.

"It is nice of you to come to our campus. Thanks for sparing some of your time. Your wife has been updating us about your work, especially the research you have done on Kautilya's *Arthashastra*."

"Madam, I am honoured that I am able to speak about my small achievements. All of this has happened due to God's grace and the blessings of so many elders," I said.

Over a cup of tea, I asked, "Is there any specific area you want me to talk about to your students?"

She replied, "If you can explain how the *Arthashastra*

has been relevant in your business and life, it will inspire our students to study Indian scriptures."

She explained further, "You are a young man and have already achieved so much. The young generation looks upon you as a role model. Do give them tips to become successful in life."

As I was taken to the auditorium, I was surprised that the hall was full. After the introduction, I was called on stage to deliver my lecture on the topic, 'Application of Chanakya's Wisdom in Modern Business'.

I started, "When I was first introduced to the *Arthashastra* by my grandfather, I had no idea that I would be standing on such a prestigious platform in a university one day to deliver a lecture on the book."

I grew emotional, "My first salutations to my grandfather, my *Guru* of the *Arthashastra* and my parents who are present here, and to the professors of the university and all my dear students." I think I struck a chord with the audience in this opening statement.

"I want to tell you that being a teacher is the greatest privilege one could be blessed with. I am happy that my wife has taken up teaching as a profession right here in the university. Frankly, I feel jealous of her, when I compare her career with mine."

All of them started laughing.

"I have been asked to tell you the story of my application of Chanakya's wisdom in my life and business. So, let me tell you that if you want to understand Chanakya's wisdom, you first need to understand Indian spirituality. Chanakya was a great teacher – a kingmaker, but most importantly, he had a good base in spirituality."

I explained, "If you want to understand Chanakya, read our other books like the *Bhagavad Gita*, the *Ramayana* and the *Upanishads*. I have been doing that since childhood and that has given me the confidence to face all the challenges of life."

I continued to speak about how I learnt the *Arthashastra* under a Sanskrit teacher in a small village, how I made the decision of becoming an entrepreneur, how it was also important to create employment opportunities and other experiences of my life.

"Instead of looking for a job, try to create jobs." I recieved a big round of applause for that statement. "Today, I have a big company with over 500 employees.

However, every time I have a challenge to overcome, I read the *Arthashastra*, and like magic, I find a solution."

I spoke for about an hour, which was followed by a question-and-answer session. Many curious questions were asked, right from how one can get a funder in business to the key reasons for success in any business.

I answered most of them, but my favourite question was when a young girl asked me, "Is it possible for a girl to manage her work and family life, and succeed in both?"

"Of course, nothing is impossible according to Chanakya." I continued, "Women are great at multitasking. In fact, men cannot do what they do. They have better emotional intelligence than men; that is why they can be successful. Make sure, however, that you enjoy motherhood as well. That is where women find fulfillment."

The audience went completely silent after this statement. I had not planned to say it, but it came spontaneously. I looked at my mother and my wife. Both had a look of appreciation for what I had said.

After my talk, the head of the department told me, "Your lecture was very good. It was very practical and useful to all of us."

As a parting thought, she suggested, "You should try to give more such lectures in order to inspire the young."

I declined, "No Madam, I am too small for that. I am not even a PhD like my wife. After all, it is her domain. Why should I enter it?"

"Then, why don't you do your PhD as well?" she countered.

My wife was smiling at me. It seemed she was speaking through this professor. I was now seriously thinking about it.

Back home, my parents were very proud of me and expressed it.

When my wife and I were alone, she cleared her throat and said, "You mentioned in your speech today about how women should enjoy motherhood... "

# 45

# The Joy of Parenting

**M**arriage is not just between two people, but also between two families. Marriages are also about children and the generations that will come after you.

"We are in the family way," Doctor said, her eyes downcast. I did not know how to respond to this news. I felt strange. I suddenly realized that I was going to be a father and Doctor was going to be a mother. I was happy, but froze as I did not know how to handle the new responsibility.

Doctor slowly looked lifted her eyes to look at me and found me dazed and confused. "Are you not happy?" she asked in surprise and concern.

"Oh yes, I am but... " I needed some time alone to think.

"But what?" she was suddenly upset.

"I mean, we are going to be parents, right?"

"Yes. We are going to be parents very soon."

I composed myself and smiled, "Wow! I can't believe it!" I nearly screamed in joy and gave her a warm hug.

Parenting is a joy, but the joy also comes with responsibility. I wanted to be a responsible parent.

That day, sitting in my office, I realized that even though I was going to be a father for the first time, I already had a big family – all the employees who were working in my company. If I was taking care of so many people already, I would be able to take care of my own kids, too.

Chanakya has given wonderful advice about parenting:

*For the first five years, love your child, for the next ten years discipline them, and after that, consider them your friends. (Chanakya Niti)*

The Lord showered us with double blessings of twins – a girl and a boy. They were almost identical, yet one could make out the difference between the two.

With the arrival of the children came many events and rituals, from the naming ceremony to various temple visits, keeping all of us busy. Even in office, my mind was really at home. I looked forward to coming home to see the kids.

The interaction between my parents and Doctor's parents increased. There were many visits from friends and relatives.

The first stage of parenting is extremely wonderful. The children believe their parents to be God. Everything you tell them, they believe to be true.

As my kids grew up, I realized that my daughter always had an upper hand over my son. She used to say, "Listen, I am elder to you by five minutes. So, treat me with respect."

During this period, I also took one of the most difficult decisions in my life – to enroll for a PhD. I now had to split the time I dedicated to each of my responsibilities three ways – to run my business, to be a good father and to study and conduct research towards my PhD.

My PhD guide was very intelligent and motherly. She understood my responsibilities at work and home and gave me quite a few tips.

"Remember, during your years of research at the university, you will be faced with two parallel activities. The first is to study and do your research well. The second is the administrative aspect, which will be required to complete the formalities. Try to balance between the two." Her tips helped me a lot.

Now that I was formally registered as a PhD student, I had to visit the university on a regular basis. It was good discipline for me. I spent a lot of time in the library, reading books and discussing with other research scholars.

I also had to attend some research methodology classes to familiarize myself with the university research framework. That is when I realized that there were other students who would accompany me on this journey.

A fellow PhD scholar asked me, "What is the topic of your research?"

"Kautilya's *Arthashastra* and its leadership philosophy – application in modern business."

He was impressed. "Wow! That seems very interesting. So, once you complete your research, I am sure you will choose to teach this topic."

At that moment, I realized that most people complete their PhD to pursue an academic career. However, I was already applying the *Arthashastra* and Chanakya's ideas in my own business. I did not need another academic career.

I also realized that, God forbid, if my business did not do as well in the future, I could become an academician and a teacher, just like my wife. So, without any planning, I already had a backup career – teaching.

"Yes, I plan to be a teacher in the long run," I said to my fellow scholar.

This phase of my career was most stressful. The demand for my time was growing on all fronts. I was working nonstop.

At times, I would be traveling across cities for business, reading books and making notes, attending board meetings and reading reports submitted by my employees – all in a day.

However, every time I came back home and the children rushed to me and uttered the words, "Papa..." all the stress would disappear. I felt re-energized. Every night, I loved to hear my kids say, "Papa, tell us a story."

The innocence of children teaches you many things. They listen to you, adore you and admire you. While narrating stories to children, you realize that it is a great way to communicate effectively with them.

It also reminds me of my own childhood when my grandparents used to tell me stories.

# 46

# Money Will Liberate You

One day, I was sitting in my office, going through the various business activities I was running. I realized that I had many companies now. Even though I was primarily into the travel business, some new businesses had emerged.

We started a bus service company. Then, we started a company where one of our services was to provide well-qualified tour guides, who knew a lot about Indian monuments and could provide detailed explanations to tourists.

As I was looking at these companies, I realized that business was very different from how I had initially thought it to be. I leaned back.

By this time, I had made a lot of money and my business was only going to get bigger. It was a great feeling that all the efforts that I had put for years together were bearing fruit.

Then, I started thinking about the philosophy of money. What exactly is money? They say money makes the world go round. The whole world bows down to money.

What is this nature of money? Moreover, the *Arthashastra* was also about money. This book survived the test of time, because it dealt with money and wealth.

I opened the book with these words:

*This science (of Arthashastra) brings into being and preserves spiritual good, material well-being and pleasures, and destroys spiritual evil, material loss and hatred. (15.1.72)*

I realized that money could give you not only material but spiritual happiness too. I wanted to discuss these thoughts with a mature person. I called up the chairman and asked him if I could meet him.

"Yes, of course, anything urgent?" he wanted to know, for my tone suggested urgency.

"Sir, I wanted to talk to you about the nature of money and wealth."

There were a few seconds of silence. Then he replied, "Come right now."

The chairman had completed his work for the day and was ready to receive me. "Let us go to the beach and talk about this."

Whenever the chairman wanted to think seriously, he liked to take a walk along the seashore. It was already evening and the best time to see the sunset too.

"Sir, tell me more about your understanding of money," I started.

"Money is a powerful tool in this world: It can do wonders; it can buy you many material objects; help you invent new objects; explore impossibilities; it can help you help others." He continued after a pause, "Money can liberate you."

I was stunned by this. " Sir, you mean spiritual liberation?" I asked.

"Yes. *Moksha…* enlightenment."

"*Moksha* through money?" I asked in disbelief.

Looking at my face, he said, "A lot of people believe that money is evil and the root cause of all the problems in the world. These people are narrow-minded," he said with visible frustration.

He added, "India was a wealthy country for so many years, and at the same time, it was a highly evolved spiritual country. Wealth supports spirituality. In poverty, one cannot really focus on God, as the mind is constantly worried only about basic survival.

On the other hand, when one has an abundance of money, he starts asking the philosophical questions of life – Who am I? Is there something beyond living and dying?"

I had come across this perspective for the first time. "All wealthy people may not necessarily be spiritual, but a wealthy person can understand spirituality differently," he explained.

Then I asked him, "Sir, will money not bring us attachment?"

He replied with a question, "Does poverty guarantee detachment?"

I continued, "Money can make you arrogant."

He replied, "The abundance of money will allow you to be more charitable."

"Money can make you greedy."

"Money can help you serve the needy."

"Sir, money is not everything."

He smiled and asked, "Is poverty a virtue?"

I was not convinced. "More money means more problems."

"More money means more freedom to choose."

"The search for money can be limitless."

He said, "Happiness should also be unlimited."

I continued asking him questions and he answered, showing me varied perspectives. Finally, after much discussion, he said something very beautiful.

"In our country, money is considered as divine. It is given the form of Goddess Laxmi. But remember, if money is not given this spiritual form, it can be harmful. Money by itself is not evil or good. It is the person who handles it."

I was somewhat convinced when he gave the example of Goddess Laxmi. "Sir, how can one divinize money?"

He was happy. "Good question. There is a method for that." He explained, "Laxmi is the wife of Lord Vishnu. Remember Lord Vishnu manages the whole world. He requires Laxmi to do that, but Laxmi is at the feet of Lord Vishnu, serving him with love and attention."

I liked the analogy. He said, "Vishnu represents knowledge and Laxmi represents wealth. If you only look at Laxmi, her husband Vishnu will get angry. If you look at Vishnu, however, Laxmi will follow. A wife goes where her husband is. Therefore, focus on knowledge and wealth will follow."

Both of us laughed at this. The sun had already set. As I came home that day, the words of this great, wealthy businessman were ringing in my ears. "Money will liberate you."

One can achieve liberation through money, too. I realized that people feel a lot of guilt about their money. For the first time, I did not feel guilty about my goal to become the richest man in the world.

I went to sleep feeling fulfilled.

# 47

# The Real Challenge

I was building my business brick by brick. There was much to learn on the way. My company was growing by leaps and bounds and was now well renowned and respected. Money was coming in; but our challenges were also increasing.

"Do you know what the most critical business challenge is?" the chairman asked me casually one day.

"Getting more and more money," I replied.

"That is an ongoing challenge in handling money. The real business challenge is to get the right kind of people to join your companies."

I had heard it said before that real secret to a thriving business is attracting and managing the right talent.

"Many people ask me the means by which I attained success in business." The chairman was giving me some real wisdom.

"Even though I give them so many different answers, I have personally realized that it is your own people who grow your business. As a business leader, you can only give direction, develop a strategy and frame policies. It is your people who will finally make you successful."

When I was referring to the *Arthashastra*, I found a chapter that detailed Chanakya's advice on how to select efficient ministers. This advice was very relevant to any business that wanted to select good managers.

Chanakya suggested looking for the following qualities in a potential minister or manager:

1.  **Desire to learn:** The person should be open-minded. After learning all the theories of management, a trainee should be able to learn the practical side from his seniors at work.

2.  **Ability to listen effectively:** Listening is hearing plus thinking. He should be able to understand what the organization expects of him.

3.  **Ability to reflect:** He should be able to look at situations from all angles. Both logical and creative thinking are required in the field of management.

4.  **Ability to reject false views:** He should be able to reach his own conclusions. He should be able to differentiate between various points of view.

5.  **Intent on the truth, not on the person:** This is the ability to separate the person from the problem. He should be able to stick to the truth that he has reached after his own careful analysis.

I was quite amazed at how Chanakya observed the psychological aspects of a person before recruiting him. I used these principles of selection and tested new trainee managers based on these qualities before recruiting them.

I was surprised at the results. There was one more technique I applied to select new managers.

Whenever I went to a college to give lectures, I would meet

many young boys and girls who wanted to join my business. I tested them and recruited many of these aspiring youngsters.

One day, a friend of mine, who also ran a big business, asked me, "How is it that people do not leave your company? While I am struggling to retain people, your employees appear loyal and committed to staying on with you. What is the secret?"

"My people do not join me as employees, they join as my students. Therefore, there is a major difference in your company and mine," I said with pride.

"In your business, people look at you as the boss. In my business, they consider me a mentor and a teacher. If your team considers you as a teacher, the commitment is lifelong."

"What about compensation?" he asked.

"Pay them well as per your capacity. Remember, however, that it is not just money that keeps people in your company. The real reason is they should feel cared for." I told him what Chanakya suggested:

*And, in all cases, he should favour the stricken (subjects) like a father. (4.4.43)*

I interpreted the verse from the *Arthashastra* for him and said, "Look upon them as your own children and you will see the magic." Even though I was considered a young business leader, I was already thinking like an old man.

I started recruiting business heads under me. The unique experience was when I recruited my first CEO who would report to me. I was a business leader, but now I had business leaders reporting to me.

The chairman had once told me, "The real business is running various businesses." I now realized that people run businesses; therefore, you need to have good people running those businesses for you.

However, you cannot treat your business heads like any other employee. They need to be given a share in the profit, freedom and also guidance. At the same time, they also have to be responsible and accountable for their businesses.

One of our companies was doing very well. So, we decided to raise more funds from the public through an Initial Public Offering (IPO).

Making various presentations to potential investors was a great learning experience for me.

During one such media interaction, a journalist asked me, "You have good business experience now. How about writing a book on your experience?"

For a moment, I was startled. "I have never thought of writing a book."

The journalist smiled back, "There is always a first time."

Was I talented enough to write a book and share my experiences? I had never wanted to, but if a journalist of repute had suggested it, I thought the idea was worth considering.

It was the birthday of my *Guru*, who had taught me the *Arthashastra*. I called him up, for it was a yearly affair to wish him.

After all the wishes, he suddenly asked me in a serious tone, "What happened to your PhD?"

# 48

# Doctor Makes a Doctor

It had been three years since I had registered for my PhD. It was only due to my wife's subtle pushing that I had gotten into the field.

Everyone aspires to be a successful person, but not many take the difficult path. In the same way, I guess every educated person also aspires to complete his PhD, which is among the highest degrees in education.

However, there is a difference between a wish and a goal. Everyone wishes to become something, but only a few turn their wish into a goal, work hard towards it and achieve it.

In the same manner, I had turned my wish of completing my PhD into a goal and had been working hard to complete it, in spite of my busy business schedule and time commitments at home. However, my progress was very slow.

One day, my guide called me and said, "Come and meet me. I need to discuss something important with you." Whenever she called me, I used to feel anxious, because I knew that as a teacher, she may point out an important tip for my research.

When I met her, she said something very interesting. "We are going to Athens in Greece." The World Congress of Philosophy was to be held in Greece that year. This was the biggest congregation of academicians, scholars and philosophers from across the globe, who would gather on one platform to discuss diverse topics.

Since I had registered for my PhD in the *Arthashastra*, I had been asked to submit a research paper based on Chanakya's philosophy of leadership.

"Your paper has been selected by the international panel of scholars and you have been invited to speak there," she said with a smile.

Greece is the cradle of Western philosophy, where thinkers like Socrates, Plato and Aristotle were born, who gave the human race a new direction.

Athens, the capital of Greece, had many historical sites like the Acropolis, from where the world still draws its inspiration. Even the Olympic Games started in Athens.

"We will go as a part of the Indian delegation. You will be part of the team." It was indeed a privilege to represent India. Eastern philosophy started from India and Western from Greece.

I was going to take our philosophy to them. After a few months of preparation, a group of academicians from all over India left for Greece.

My research paper presentation was well appreciated by the international scholar community. We also made friends with scholars from other countries.

I was surprised that the academic world was very big and connected. More than 100 countries participated in the World Congress through more than 5,000 delegates. My eyes had opened to a new world altogether.

On the way back in the plane, my guide told me, "Make sure you complete your PhD at the earliest. Another world will open up to you."

I had decided that I would complete my research in the next six months. Come what may, I wanted to achieve this goal in the set time.

The next step was to submit my synopsis – the outcome of my years of research. Once that was approved, I had to submit my final thesis. The final step was to attend an interview panel called the viva voce. After I cleared that, I would be conferred with my doctoral degree.

My research journey was almost racing towards the finish line. As in a marathon race, it was necessary to speed up towards the end.

As I was moving forward, I was also looking back on how the PhD journey had started. During the journey, I had gained many insights into the process of obtaining a PhD.

My first lesson was that a PhD was not like most other courses in the Indian education system, where a person had to appear for exams and the marks determined the future of the candidate. In fact, after registering for a PhD, there are no formal exams. It is all about research and its outcome.

The second lesson I learnt was the importance of the tuning between the research scholar and the research guide. It is a very intense journey.

It is a *Guru-Shishya* relationship, where the student gains from the guide's years of academic experience and the guide gives direction to the student's endeavors to complete his research.

I had submitted my final thesis and was sitting in my viva voce session. Apart from my guide, an external scholar from another university had evaluated my research work.

Over the course of the two-hour viva, I was asked questions on all possible aspects of my research. The objective was to assess what value my research outcome would add to the academic world.

At the end of the two hours, the other scholar said, "Good work, doctor. We will let you know the result soon." I was asked to wait outside the room.

While going out, my guide smiled at me, and I suddenly realized that the other panelist had called me a 'Doctor'. It was a subtle hint that I had cleared the final step. However, the rules did not permit them to tell me the result verbally. I had to wait for a written confirmation. I knew, however, that I had done it.

In the next few months, after all the formalities, I received a letter and was called for the convocation ceremony to receive my doctoral degree. I only thanked my wife for her support. One doctor had made another doctor.

Doctor looked at me and said with satisfaction, "Congratulations, doctor. Now that you have cleared the first goal in academics, when will you achieve your next target?"

What was my next target?

# 49

# From Scholar to Author

The world of academics is very strange. I thought obtaining a PhD was the completion of an academic journey. However, I realized that it was the beginning of yet another journey.

I had gone to thank my guide for her continuous support during my research. I realized that my children had grown up from toddlers to the age when they asked all kinds of questions.

Whenever they asked me about how the world worked, it seemed to me that they were asking questions pertaining to my research.

The four years of my doctoral research had brought out a different person in me. I had learnt not to accept anything without the clarity of thought. It is a good mindset. It teaches you the right way of thinking – *Aanvikshiki*.

This mindset remains with you for life. Your PhD title also remains for life. For the rest of your life, you will be addressed as "Doctor" and not "Mr" or "Ms" any longer. The world respects you as a scholar of repute and looks at you from a different perspective.

"PhD is a new vision of life. It is like a new window through which you look at the world outside," said my guide.

"Many new possibilities will open up before you. Remember to keep your eyes and ears open. Make sure you grab the opportunity when it arrives."

She narrated her own experience. "I did not have any idea of what a doctoral degree could do to me. My own research guide had told me this. I was an average person, but due to his guidance, I am in this university and guiding future generations of scholars and thinkers."

I was quite amazed when she shared her experiences.

"I have travelled across the globe, been on various expert committees of the government, formed education policies and contributed to the building of knowledge," she said with pride.

Something in me wanted more convincing. I asked her, "Is it not enough to be a teacher? Is that not a noble profession? What if one just continues as a teacher, without a PhD degree?"

"There is no doubt that teaching by itself is a noble profession in which one guides students. But having a PhD degree helps you to impact not just students, but the education system as a whole."

I understood where she came from. There are millions of teachers in schools and colleges across the globe, but only a few of them complete their formal PhD education and then we see that they contribute differently.

I also remembered the incident of my *Arthashastra Guru*, when I had gone for a conference and the chief minister had requested him to give a lecture to the cabinet ministers.

The chief minister must have known various teachers, but then, an expert like my *Guru* is different. Why did he invite only my *Guru* to speak and not the other teachers he knew? My *Guru* was a rare expert in the field of knowledge.

An expert is always in demand and a PhD degree makes

you an expert in your field of research. "You have achieved a PhD in the *Arthashastra*. Now go and spread the knowledge of your research to the world. This is your next target," my guide instructed me.

Before I could speak, she continued, "I know you are a busy man, with your business and many responsibilities, but take out some time from your busy schedule and make sure you connect with the youth of the country. They require a role model like you."

These were not just suggestions from my guide; for me, they were instructions. "Also, keep writing research papers, at least one in six months. And if possible, do write a book on your experiences," she added.

After a long discussion, as I left the room, she smiled at me. "Keep coming to the university. Do not disappear after getting your PhD."

I nodded and she said, "Remember, getting a PhD is not the end of the journey, but the beginning of a bigger journey, a journey that never ends."

After the completion of my research, I felt a big burden had lifted off my shoulders. Now, I was ready to shoulder higher responsibilities.

While I was attending a meeting in office one day, a sales manager said to his team members, "The best way to grow business is to use leverage. If I can reach ten people, using leverage, I can reach a hundred more. Remember to use leverage to grow in life."

I was suddenly struck with an idea. What leverage could I use to convey my research findings to the greatest number of people? If I were to lecture individually, I would be able to reach students in say, a thousand colleges.

Was there a way to reach millions by just by sitting at one place? Then, I realized the best way to leverage in the field of knowledge was by writing a book based on my research.

Many people read books, and even those who cannot meet you personally can gain from your wisdom through your writings. In fact, books last even beyond the death of the writer.

How else would Chanakya convey his knowledge to our generation? He had the vision to document his experiences and findings in the *Arthashastra*.

If Chanakya had not written the *Arthashastra*, we would have lost his wisdom forever. Inspired by the great Chanakya, I decided to write a book myself. The scholar in me wanted to be a writer.

I did not know the world of publishing, but my next target was set – to write a book, a bestseller.

# 50

# Writing a Bestseller

"The best way to write a book is to write it." I read this in a book I referred to while I was preparing to write my first book. I was not sure how books were written or how the publishing industry worked; but I was determined to write a book.

One of my business clients was a member of an elite club. From time to time, they invited external speakers to discuss different topics with their club members. This client once asked me if I could address them on the topic of "Chanakya and his relevance in modern business." I agreed.

When I went to speak there, I realized that the group consisted of the richest businessmen in our city. They were from various backgrounds.

There was full attendance to listen to the wisdom of Chanakya. I think I impressed them quite a bit during my half-hour talk. Discussions continued after the talk too.

An elderly gentleman came to me after the talk. "Young man, you speak well. Would you want to try writing a book on your subject?" I was taken aback, because I had been thinking about how to publish a book for quite some time.

He gave me his visiting card and I realized that he was the chairman of one of India's biggest publishing houses. I was awed. Thousands of people might approach his company to get their books published, but only a few get through. And here, by the grace of the Lord, such a big man was asking me to write a book.

"Of course, Sir," was my immediate answer.

"Let us meet in my office with my editorial team," he suggested.

The following week, I went to his office and three people were part of the meeting. The editorial team was quite friendly.

One of them, who had also come to attend my talk, began, "Sir, we were quite impressed by your speech that day. You have tremendous grip over your subject. As our chairman has requested, we want to explore the possibility of you writing a book with us on the same subject."

I was happy yet hesitant. "Thank you for your kind approach. I am happy to work on this project. However, let me confess that I have no background of how to write a book and what it takes to make a book happen."

"That is what we are here for," they smiled. "That should be the least of your concerns. We always look forward to potential good writers, who can add value to our publishing house. Your topic of expertise – Kautilya's *Arthashastra* and its application in modern businesses – looks very good for us."

That made me more confident of taking up this project. Another young girl of the editorial team joined in, "Sir, we have done a little bit of research about you. Apart from running various businesses, you have also completed your PhD on Chanakya."

"Yes, that is right," I said with a sense of pride. I remembered what my PhD guide had said, that I would be in a different league after completing my PhD.

"Can we look at your PhD thesis to begin with?" the chief editor asked.

"That should not be a problem," I said.

The chairman also joined the discussion. "This is good. You already have some experience in writing. It does not matter if you have not written a book, but the experience of research and writing a thesis helps."

I sent my thesis to them. After a week, I got a call from the editorial team. "Sir, is it all right if we publish your PhD thesis as a book?" I was pleasantly shocked.

"Your thesis is simple and easy to understand for the lay reader. We realized that if it is refined a bit, it can be a good book," the editor added.

What else does a first-time author want? First, the chairman of a publishing company approaches you; next, the chief editor says that something you wrote in the past is good to be converted into a book. I realized that I did not have to write a book from scratch at all. It was ready material.

During the next few months, we refined my thesis and converted it into a good-looking book. The publishing company also priced it such that it was quite affordable for readers.

When the first cut of the book came into my hands, it was an emotional moment for me. It felt like I was holding my children when they were just born.

I may never physically give birth to a child as a mother, but I could relate to what every mother feels after her first child is born.

A mother who had just delivered her baby described the

feeling well, "A part of me got separated, yet it made me complete."

I asked my publishers, "The book is ready now. How do we make it a bestseller?"

"For that, we need to reach a minimum of 10,000 copies in sales," said the chairman.

As a businessman, no sales figure was too big for me. "Is that all? I will be able to reach that figure all by myself. Let us target a bigger number," I said confidently.

In the next few months, the book was launched in a grand ceremony at the university, attended by more than 300 people. I also promoted the book aggressively. I did book events in over 14 cities. Finally, we reached a sales figure of one lakh copies.

The book became a national bestseller, going into over 50 reprints. This was also thanks to the media, who gave favorable reviews.

Smiling, the editor asked me, "When will you write your next book?"

# 51

# The Wonderful Feeling of Freedom

Books make you famous. A bestselling book makes you very famous. The first book was quite an effort for me, because I was trying to understand how the publishing industry worked.

I need to thank my publishers, for after working with them closely, I understood the game very well now.

In the next five years, I had written three books. All of them turned out to be bestsellers.

A television journalist asked me in a live interview, "How do you write bestseller after bestseller?"

I smiled and said, "I write books and make sure they are bestsellers." The dynamics of books and the publishing industry had changed over the years. I realized that marketing and branding was the key to success.

You may have a good book, but if you do not market it well, the book will remain in some corner of a bookstore, lying unnoticed, dying its own natural death.

However, with continuous activities around the book, people notice it, discuss it, recommend it to others, and it is finally this word of mouth that makes a book a bestseller.

Around this time, a well-known film company approached me and said they would like to make a movie on my first book. I was quite surprised, because that was a management book and I could not understand how a movie could be made on it.

The producer assured me, "Don't worry about that. We know how to make films; it is our business. Just say yes."

I gave her the go-ahead.

Within a year, a management film was made on my first book. It was much appreciated in business schools in India and abroad. It also went on to win some international film festival awards. Soon, several people were approaching me to make films and television serials based on my other books too.

Life was taking a new turn. I was living in a dream world. Fame, money, glory, everything was coming to me naturally. During this time, someone asked me, "What is your next goal in life?"

My answer surprised him, "I have no goals. All my goals have been fulfilled. What else can I ask God for?" In the fullest sense, I had everything – a growing business, a loving family, intelligent children and many good friends.

However, another interesting development was that many rich businessmen began seeking my advice. Most of them were richer than me and senior to me in age and experience.

I once asked a rich businessman, "Sir, I am younger to you in age, and you have more experience than me in business. Then why do you come to me?"

He said, "You have one thing that I do not have... "

"What?" I wanted to know.

"The working knowledge of Chanakya's wisdom."

It was true. I was indirectly practicing Chanakya and the

*Arthashastra* in every walk of life. As a teacher, businessman and an advisor, I was doing what Chanakya had suggested.

Many companies and business organizations began inviting me for keynote lectures. It helped me to understand business from a more holistic perspective. The combination of a PhD degree and a bestselling author status ensured that I was invited for numerous lectures.

One day, the chairman of a company, who attended my lecture, said, "Sir, I know you are a busy man, but would you like to join the advisory board of my company? It will help me give direction to my business."

He continued, "I will also make you a shareholder in my company. Rest assured that I will compensate you well for your time and valuable advice."

I had never thought that I could become the owner of someone else's business just by giving advice.

I opened a commentary of the *Arthashastra* by a great scholar, to find a direction. It said:

**Wealth is not only what is 'with' you but also what is 'in' you.**

I had grown inside. I did not know my own value until someone else pointed it out to me. I closed my eyes and thanked God for such a blessed life.

That day, when I was reading the *Bhagavad Gita*, I realized that the ultimate aim of a successful businessman was to serve the society, not just to hoard wealth and be greedy for more money.

Finally, I gave up my last desire – to become the richest man in the world. I felt free. I did not want anything else. I had entered a state of being free from desire. I found that I felt fulfilled and complete.

Yet, I had to work in this world to guide others towards a higher, purposeful life. I began advising other people on how to apply Chanakya's wisdom and turn around their business the Chanakya way.

One may wonder about the fate of my own growing business house, when I was spending most of my time in guiding other businessmen.

My various businesses were now handled by several of my team members, CEOs and other managers. I had developed the knack of getting work done through others. I was only giving strategic advice to others and to the people running my own businesses.

There is a saying that "When your desire ends, God fulfills his desires through you." It seemed that the Almighty wanted me to become the richest man in the world, even though that did not interest me at all.

Sometimes, you find the way, and sometimes, the way finds you...

# 52

# The Leader in Me

Time teaches you everything. I was young no more, and people elder to me were getting older.

My chairman's health had been deteriorating for some time. In the last few years, the group companies had grown by leaps and bounds.

My own travel business was showing tremendous growth year after year and was among the best performing companies in the group.

One day, the chairman called me home. He was in bed and the doctor had just attended to him. "I have lived my life very well," he began. By that, I knew he had called me to say something very important.

"The doctor just advised me to be careful with my health. I know, my time to leave this planet is not far," he continued.

"My father handed over this business to me and I did my best to make it grow. I am happy that I did my role well," he said, satisfied. "Now, I have a last duty – to appoint the next chairman after me."

He recollected his past. "For many years, our group company

was handed over from one generation to another within the family. But the time has come for a big change."

He looked into my eyes and said, "Times have changed and we are now a professionally run business house. Therefore, for the first time, we want the next chairman to be someone who is capable of running this large Indian multinational – not just based on the family he was born in, but on performance."

He came to the point, "I want you to be the next chairman of our group." He paused and I was in complete silence.

The chairman was unmarried. He believed that he was married to his business and all the employees were his own children.

Everyone thought that one of his relatives would succeed him to the leadership position, but we did not know who that person would be. He could choose from his various cousins and their children, all of whom were highly qualified and capable. However, the chairman had chosen me over the others.

He recollected with a smile, "The first time I called you to my office to interview you, I knew I had a potential leader in you. You were a good prince, who could be molded into a king. However, I wanted to test you. Let me tell you, in every test I conducted, you came out with flying colors."

I then recollected what Chanakya had said in the *Arthashastra*:

**He (the king) should strive to impart training to the prince. (5.6.39)**

The chairman had trained me well. I was happy that he considered me a king in training. "I will make the formal announcement in the next board meeting," the chairman concluded.

I had never imagined that such a big position would ever come to me. I felt that more than the position coming my way, I had a bigger responsibility to handle.

"Don't worry. I am sure you can handle it well. The future of our group is safe in your hands," the chairman assured me.

I had my doubts, but I had never doubted his wisdom or his knack of spotting talent. I kept quiet.

My chairman attended the next board meeting with a lot of difficulty, because his health was worsening. Most of us knew that this would be his last board meeting, and he would formally announce the next chairman.

I was not sure how the other board members would react to the announcement of my name. However, I was pleasantly surprised when all of them started clapping in joy. The best part was that not a single person was against me.

I had decided that even if one person objected to me becoming the leader, despite the chairman's recommendation I would opt out. However, I had nothing left to say or do. "We are all with you," the group had decided.

Things were different in the days to come. I took over as the new and the youngest chairman of the group with mixed feelings. At one end, I was taking charge of the new role; and on the other, my chairman, who had guided me to this role as his own son, was counting his days.

It happened one afternoon. I was in office and the phone rang, "Sir, he is gone."

I did not know how to respond. Death is a natural part of life. We all knew that the chairman's days were coming to an end. Yet, one cannot stop the upsurge of emotions in such moments.

Sitting in the chairman's office which was now my office, I

cried like a baby. This was the office from where he had guided and mentored me for years. From today, there was no one to guide me. There was no one to whom I could take my difficult questions about business and life. Who would guide me now?

My eyes fell on the table calendar, which had quotes of Swami Vivekananda with his picture. The quote for the day read:

*"The day the father dies, the son becomes a man."*

I had no guide from now; I had to guide others in business. I had taken charge as a chairman, but I realized I needed to take up a new role – that of a mentor and guide, keeping my eyes and ears open for the next prince....

# 53

# The Family Man

My children were growing and were now in college. My parents and wife were doing a fantastic job of bringing them up with the right spiritual background.

It has been said, "Give your children values first and then valuables."

My children were born with a silver spoon in their mouths. They were living in luxury. I guess every generation improves upon its previous generation's work.

Even though I was born in a middle-class family, with my business background, my family had now evolved into a high-income family.

For me, however, high or middle-class was not an economic category; I valued people more from their spiritual development.

A person born in a rich family can be poor in his spiritual foundations, and even a poor person can be spiritually evolved.

Like me, my children were also brought up in a spiritual environment. Reading the *Bhagavad Gita* and understanding the *Upanishads*, listening to the stories of great men like Rama or Krishna was natural to their upbringing.

My kids had an advantage over my childhood. I had to go to my native place every year to meet my grandparents. Because my parents stayed with me, my kids had the advantage of having their grandparents always available to them.

My wife was committed to the teaching profession in the university, and over the years, had got very good recognition in the academic field. She too started writing books and her readers appreciated her work.

Being the chairman of a multinational company with diversified operations across the globe took a lot of my time. However, I made sure I was a family man too. I used to strive for a work-life balance whenever possible.

Let me admit that it was not always possible, due to the various responsibilities of the company. Yet, whenever I had the time, I spent quality time with my family. As Chanakya had said, when children grow up, treat them as equals.

Even though my children lived luxurious lives, we made sure they understood that it was not to be taken for granted. They had to succeed in their lives on their own merits.

One day, when my children were sitting with me, my daughter asked, "Papa, what makes a person really successful?"

I was surprised and wanted to know why she had asked such a question.

"No papa, you tell me first – what makes a person successful in life?"

I thought a little and replied, "A person can become successful due to various reasons, but my experience says it is a combination of three factors – hard work, teamwork and God's grace."

My son joined the discussion. "Can you explain this some more, Papa?"

"When you start, you have to work very hard. Later in life, you realize that hard work alone is not enough. Then, you start working with others and realize the importance of teamwork."

I continued, "When you look back at your journey dispassionately, you wonder about the reason for your success. You realize that many unknown factors helped you to reach the top of the success ladder. Those unknown factors that make you successful are called God's grace."

My daughter continued to ask, "Does destiny play a major role in success?"

I got philosophical. "Destiny is another name for God's grace. If you choose to do God's work, all the power in the world comes to your assistance."

"Papa, how has your journey in business been?" She quizzed.

"For me, my business journey has been a spiritual journey," I replied.

I realized she was writing all of this in a book. "Why are you writing this?" I wanted to know.

Doctor and my parents started laughing. Doctor explained, "Your daughter has a project in college. They have to study a successful person and analyze the reasons for their success." With a smile, she added, "And she chose you for her project."

My daughter was angry. "Mummy, I told you not to tell him about the project."

I was happy that my children considered me a successful person. "Don't worry; you can ask me anything. I am ready to answer whatever you ask for your project."

In the coming years, my daughter used these notes as the basis for her first book, *My Father's Success Tips.*

You may want to teach your children, but children should also be ready to learn from you. When that happens, your experience is easily transferred to your next generation.

I have realized that children learn from what you do, rather than what you say. You cannot deceive them. They will catch you soon. What you think, you must say; and what you say, you must do.

Another important aspect of the family is that the more people there are in the family, the better it is for the children to learn from.

Our joint family system gives children the opportunity to learn from different generations and relatives.

I had analyzed my kids' horoscopes when they were little, so I knew that they were intelligent enough to choose their own careers. I also knew that unlike me, they had no interest in business and creating wealth.

Children need to be shown their strengths, but they should also have the freedom to choose their paths.

One day, my son told me, "Papa, I want to take up a government job."

This came as a shock to me.

# 54

# Choosing Your Own Path

As a businessman, I had dealt very closely with the government and politicians. I am not judging whether politicians are good or bad. Neither am I saying that the government and its rules are bad.

My view was that the government's world is very different from that of a businessman. We all live in our own little worlds. A businessman like me has all the freedom to choose the kind of life I wanted, but the government dealt in the world of rules and regulations.

By this time, I had many close friends in the government. I was not sure whether my son was aware of the world he was getting into.

I asked him plainly, "Of the many choices available to you, why do you want to take up a government job?"

"Not just any government job, Papa, I want to get into the Indian Foreign Services (IFS)," he said with pride.

"Please explain," I said. I always believed that I wanted my children to choose their careers, but when the time for that came, it seemed I was becoming a hurdle for them.

"Papa, there are many ways of serving our great

country. One of the best ways is being in public service."
He continued,

"Today, the world has become a global village. Countries
are interconnected, and we need to showcase our culture in the
best possible manner. I feel I can serve my country by being an
IFS officer, an ambassador of our great Indian culture."

"So you want to be a bureaucrat?" I almost disliked the idea.

"Why not?" He shot back, his temper rising. "Does not
Kautilya's *Arthashastra* talk about the importance of envoys
in Book One, Chapter 16?"

I was dumbfounded at my son's reference to the book that
was my guide in life. I had taught the *Arthashastra* to many
people and practiced it at every stage of life; but I had never
imagined that one day, it would come back to me through the
eyes of my children.

Before I could react, he brought his copy of the *Arthashastra*.
"Here Papa, see what Chanakya says regarding the duties of
an envoy and diplomat."

*Sending communications, guarding the terms of a treaty,*
*upholding his king's majesty, acquisition of allies,*
*instigation, dividing the enemy's friends, conveying*
*secret agents and troops into the enemy territory...*
*(1.16.33)*

"You see papa, ever since you introduced me to the
*Arthashastra* as a child, this chapter always stayed in my mind.
Look at the strategic role of an envoy." I was listening as he
talked.

"I want to serve my country in this manner. I want to be
a major part of the global game India will be playing in the

future," he concluded.

Both of us were silent for some time. I was allowing myself to recover from the shock my son had given me. He broke the silence. "If you do not agree, I will not do it." I could almost see tears in his eyes.

I was deeply moved. "No, son, I am not saying you should not join the government. I only hope that you have thought through all the aspects of your choice." That was my advice to him.

"Papa, ever since I was a child, I only dreamt of this role for myself. I have been preparing for the Civil Services exams to become an IFS officer." He showed me how he had prepared for the upcoming competitive exams.

He continued, "Papa, you have been my role model. I have always adored you. Like you, I too have loved Chanakya and his ideas. Now, I want to take this role as my career in life."

I realized that each generation is smarter than the previous one. He had done his homework well. He knew he wanted to pursue this career. I did not demotivate him anymore; neither did I become a burden.

"Make sure you speak to your mother and take the blessings of your grandparents too," I smiled.

He smiled back, "I did that long ago. You are the last person whose blessings I had to seek for the upcoming exams."

I realized that I was almost out of tune with my family and kids. However, I wanted him to give his best shot at the exams. "My blessings... you always have my blessings." We hugged each other.

I was feeling proud to be the father of a son like him. However, another thought struck me. I asked him, "Has your sister also decided her career?"

"What, Papa? You are asking me as if you did not know!"

I seemed like an absolute fool. Both my children had decided their career and future, but I was disconnected from their choices. Instead of blaming them, I realized my mistake and admitted, "No, I am not aware of it. What is the future she has chosen?"

"Go and ask her. Let her tell you."

Like a frightened mouse, I started searching for my daughter. I found her in her room, sitting quietly in a corner.

As I entered noiselessly, she looked at me and said, "So Papa, your handsome son has already told you what he wants to do. You have come here to find out my choice of career, right?"

She said with pride, "I want to be an artist."

# 55

# Be Certain

I knew my daughter was a good painter. She also sang well and had learnt two classical dance forms, Bharatanatyam and Kuchipudi.

"Which art form have you decided to pursue?" I enquired.

"Music," she replied unhesitatingly. "I want to spend a few more years studying it in depth." She detailed her plan.

"There are a few schools in India which train in the traditional format. I need to go to one of these traditional singing experts and study in a *Gurukul* format."

The word '*Gurukul*' brought back my own journey of studying the *Arthashastra*. It had changed my life completely.

"I have found out the details of this *Gharana* in Rajasthan. This old *Guruji* is a living legend. I will learn under him for a year. I can also complete my master's degree in the subject and plan to do PhD in the field of music."

My generation did not have such clarity while choosing our careers. Our children are born in a different era and are definitely much ahead of us in planning and execution.

With the realization that I was not in touch with the realities of my own home, I had mixed feelings that day. I was sad that

I had not noticed that my children had become young adults. I was also happy that they were thinking independently.

My Doctor could sense my thoughts. "Is it not good?" she asked, indicating that such career choices had made me what I am today.

"Hmm..." I smiled at her.

Both of us were fans of Kahlil Gibran and his book, *The Prophet*. Whenever there was a difference of opinion between our children and us, she had the habit of reading out his lines:

*Your children are not your children.*
*They are the sons and daughters of Life's longing for itself.*
*They come through you but not from you,*
*And though they are with you, yet they belong not to you.*

These lines have a deep spiritual meaning. I composed myself and was back to my usual self, feeling proud of my children.

Most parents in India are worried about their children. However, instead of worrying, one should be concerned about their kids. There is a difference between being worried and concerned. Worrying is like a rocking chair; it moves, but does not progress. Concern is genuine love and comes from a feeling of responsibility.

What should the role of a concerned parent be at such a critical juncture in the life of his children? As usual, I opened the *Arthashastra* and found Chanakya guiding me:

**All undertakings should be preceded by consultation.**
**Holding a consultation with only one, he may not be**

*able to reach a decision in difficult matters. With more councilors it is difficult to reach decisions and maintain secrecy. (1.15.2, 35, 40)*

I realized that the best way to guide my children was by consulting experts in the fields they had chosen. I made a list of three of India's best, retired IFS officers and another list of three successful singers. Then, I went to meet them, taking my children along.

It is said that there are three types of people in this world. The first make mistakes and learn. The second keep making mistakes and never learn. The third category is the best – those who learn from others' mistakes.

These experts guided my children on their chosen career paths. The wisdom of these experienced and successful people was so valuable that even I learnt a lot from them during these discussions.

I applied this technique in my own business as well. Whenever I had to develop a new line of business, I would make a list of three experts and seek their advice. I realized that this helped me to avoid many pitfalls, even before I had started the journey.

My children had the advantage of not having to worry about economic problems. They were lucky to be born to a rich father. They did not have to worry about making money. They just had to follow their passion. I had saved enough for my children to enable them to have a good lifestyle. I was doing my duty as a father.

However, my kids seemed smarter than I was. They clearly told Doctor and me, "The wealth you have is your creation, but we will create our own."

I was happy that they lived a simple life and treated money with respect. I could observe that they were not spendthrifts.

As I was feeling blessed, God seemed to continue to shower his blessings upon me. The company was doing extremely well and growing rapidly. We now had more than a hundred businesses and over three lakh employees. We had offices and projects running in almost every country in the world.

I was suddenly in the limelight for different reasons. I began getting recognition for my business acumen through prestigious awards such as the "Businessman of the Year", "Leader in Business" and so on.

I was invited to be part of the Prime Minister's panel for industrial development. I even travelled as part of the Indian government's delegation to various countries. I was able to help in the formation of many good business policies.

And then, one day, the magic happened. I got a call from one of my executive assistants.

"Sir, did you read the newspaper today?" He asked excitedly.

"No, what is it?" I wanted to know.

"Sir... Sir..."

# 56

# Did I Do It?

I was at home, getting ready to go to office. "Which newspaper are you talking about?"

"Sir, look at any newspaper, the headlines are the same!" the executive assistant almost shouted.

He seemed too excited to make much sense. I went to get a copy of the newspaper that was near the table. No one had touched it, because everyone was busy with their morning routines.

I saw my photo on the front page declaring me as...

Suddenly, my daughter emerged from her room, screaming, "Papa, did you see the newspaper?" She was holding another newspaper, which she had taken to her room.

"It says a well-known magazine has declared you the richest man in India."

I was dumbstruck. I started reading the newspaper and found that some survey had declared me the richest living man in our country.

For a moment, my mind went back to the days when it was my dream and I was working towards it. Many years ago, however, after I had understood the realities of money, this goal had automatically ceased to exist for me.

For me, money was just a matter of numbers that go up and down. Just because my money was known to the world did not mean that there were other people who were not richer than me. In short, what the world was considering a big achievement was not at all exciting for me.

At the same time, I realized that I should not degrade others who had a similar dream. Was I not like them when I started my journey many years ago?

It is said that money is not everything, but earn money before you can say this. I had achieved my goal, and I can say with confidence that there are many things money can do, and many that it cannot.

However, in no measure should one reject money and its importance in human life and society.

The phones kept ringing and congratulatory messages kept pouring in through the next few weeks. More of my interviews appeared in the media and I received more invitations to speak about my success story in various forums.

Most journalists had a standard question, to which I had a standard answer. They asked, "What made you the richest man?"

My answer was, "I have always invested in people. Whenever I found good people running a potentially successful business, I invested in their companies. With their growth came my growth."

It was true that apart from running my own company as a chairman, I did consider young boys and girls with innovative ideas.

I explored their business acumen and invested in them and

their companies. Not all the companies I invested in became successful, yet the ones that achieved success more than made up for the losses in the other companies. Overall, I was always a big winner.

I not only invested financially in these companies, but also gave a lot of time to guide and mentor their promoters, the way my own chairman had done at the beginning of my career.

This involvement in guiding a company from the idea stage to achieving financial success was the true reason for my success. By this time, I had understood how investment worked, and it became a game for me. First, you run behind money, and then money runs behind you.

I was not only earning money, but also giving it back in a big way. Most of my money was spent on supporting social causes. I especially loved to spend on research activities.

I loved to spend on those who had committed themselves to research in various fields. My research on the *Arthashastra* had made me understand what good research could do to oneself and the world at large.

One of my friends in college had left for the USA to pursue higher studies and research. "It is better to have brain drain, than brain in the drain," he had once said to me.

However, things had changed over the years. India had become a research-centric country, which had given birth to many innovations. Funds were pumped into research activities, not just by individuals but by the government too.

At one point, I even headed a committee set up by the government of India to encourage innovation at the grassroots level, as well as in various schools and colleges. That work gave me the most satisfaction.

Some people called me a philanthropist, some a venture capitalist, some a funder of new ideas, some a supporter of innovation. The reality was that I was working closely with the youth of India and with their billion-dollar ideas.

The youth of India did not fail me.

However, the institution that I loved to fund for research was the same *Ashram* where I had studied and researched on Kautilya's *Arthashastra*.

Over the years, it had become a modern *Ashram* with very good facilities for modern-day academic research. Like me, thousands of students had done various research projects on Indology and worked on taking ancient Indian wisdom to a global platform.

Then, one day, as a natural growth of all my business investments, I was declared "The richest man in the world!" Did I do it all by myself? I had to thank Chanakya for all this.

A famous international magazine that compiled the list of richest men in the world did a cover story on me with my photo on its cover page.

The caption to my photo read, "A noble businessman...."

# 57

# I Find Myself

I had started realizing that as you grow bigger, an unseen force is working with you. At one point, I had even lost count of how many businesses I was involved in. The growth was uncontrollable and unstoppable.

People felt I was working very hard for the growth of such a big business group. In reality, however, I was becoming a non-doer. I was working hard in the external world, but inside, a sense of detachment was growing.

I felt that after achieving all that one wants, one should seek spiritual growth. I was not too old. I was healthy. Yet, I decided to take an untimely decision – to retire from the post of chairman.

When I expressed this desire to my board members, they were taken aback. They expected me to continue for at least another 10 years. "Why so early?" "Are there any problems?" they asked.

"No problems at all. I have done my work well and would like to leave with a sense of satisfaction." I really meant my words. All the businesses were on autopilot. We had a very good second-level leadership team in place.

The big question for the board was who the next chairman would be. Long ago, I had identified a young girl from my previous chairman's family, his sister's daughter, as a potential leader.

The brilliant girl that she was, I always believed that she had fantastic business sense in her DNA. Having studied in one of the best business schools, her mindset was par excellence. I had started applying Chanakya's wisdom on her:

*When the prince is ready for it (knowledge), experts should train him. (1.17.27)*

The only difference was that this time, it was not a prince but a princess.

I had trained her and groomed her. I knew she was ready to take up the position. She would be the first woman to helm this century-old business group.

The age of women's leadership had arrived. This was also a message to society that we truly believed in that leadership.

Most of the board members agreed with my choice. Some had their doubts, but I knew that they could not oppose me directly, because under my leadership, the company had grown manifold.

I took them into confidence, "Believe me, time will prove that this is the best decision I have ever taken."

It was my last day in office. I was sitting quietly after preparing for the next day's program of the new leader's formal takeover. I looked at my chairman's photo kept on my table.

"Sir, I hope I have done what you wanted me to do," I asked my inspiration and business mentor. I was feeling a sense of gratitude towards this great man who made me what I am today.

On a similar day many years ago, he had trusted me as the first non-family member to take over his leadership role. Today, I was handing the business back to the family.

There was a knock on the door. The new chairman, or should we say, Chairwoman entered. She sat down quietly in front of me. I could see her emotions. I did not speak and wanted her to start the conversation.

After a few moments, she said, "Sir, thank you for choosing me over my brother."

That was the first time I realized that her biggest problem was not whether she had confidence in her capability, but if she would get a chance as a woman leader.

As I was going to end my role as a business leader, I had learnt a very hard lesson about the society we live in.

Women were still not given the equal opportunity they deserved. Especially in business families, which were dominated by men over various generations, it was difficult to break the mold.

Without realizing it, I had become a trendsetter with my final decision.

Looking into my eyes, she said, "Sir, I will never let you down." I knew she would not.

Then, she asked a question that set me thinking. "What is the best advice you would give me as a leader?"

I replied spontaneously, "The day you retire, while choosing your next leader, follow your gut." Both of us had a hearty laugh.

That evening, when I sat for my daily meditation, I was able to concentrate naturally, effortlessly. I was at ease with myself.

A great man has said, "Meditation is not a process, but a state of mind." I was feeling meditative. I was feeling relaxed. I was getting more and more comfortable with myself.

That night, I went through a divine spiritual experience.

Rumi, the Sufi mystic has said, "You are not a drop in the ocean. You are the entire ocean in a drop." I experienced it that night.

My consciousness expanded. I felt limitless. I knew I had broken all the mental barriers that nobody but I had created. My body seemed to be different from me. I knew that I was not in the body, but the body was in me.

In that state of awareness, I sat quietly, doing nothing, just being myself. For the first time, I understood what it meant to be called enlightened. I had realized my true self.

I had attained Nirvana... Moksha... the state of *Jeevan Mukti*. I had achieved the real purpose of human birth.

The game was over. The dancer and the dance had become one. No duality remained. The difference between the inside and the outside ceased to exist. Everything merged into me. I dissolved into myself, forever.

My mind had become – no mind....

# 58

# My Later Life

There are different understandings of the word Moksha or self-realization. Many consider that it is attained only after death.

However, with my own experience, I realized that it is natural to everyone. We are not human beings on a spiritual journey, but spiritual beings on a human journey.

Our *Upanishads* and other scriptures have discussed this in detail. I had studied them since my childhood, but for the first time, the theory of *"Aham Brahma asmi"* ("I am Brahman") had become a practical living experience for me.

One may wonder what happens after a person attains self-realization. What does that person do later?

Your perspective of life changes entirely. Your vision in life becomes completely different. Everything becomes a divine play. You no more work for happiness. You work from happiness. You attain a desire-less state of mind.

So, does such a person become lazy?

No, in fact, it is the other way round. After self-realization, you become active in the world outside in entirely different ways.

Before self-realization, one worked to achieve some selfish goals. Now, you work for the larger benefit of the society. You slowly start guiding others towards the spiritual happiness you have found yourself.

I too became fully active with full awareness, but the type of activity was different. I was no more involved in business, but got involved in various other social and spiritual activities.

I did not leave my family, but my family had expanded. I felt the whole world had become my family.

I continued to work with more rigor. I had a big advantage. Because I had a lot of money, I started looking for projects that required money. I started donating more and more. However, more wealth continued to come to me unasked.

The more I gave, the more I got. However, there was no sense of ownership. I was used as an instrument of the Lord to do more and more good work.

My son topped the IFS exams, and after training, was posted to many foreign countries where he contributed to building strong international relations. He was truly happy and enjoyed his job.

India was growing economically and he was instrumental in creating many good foreign policies for our country. His work was recognized well in government circles, both in our country and internationally.

My daughter completed her PhD in music and went on to become a full-time singer. The best part was that not only did she continue sharpening her skills as a singer, but she also started her own music school.

She encouraged new singers to take up the profession. She ran a *Gurukul* in the traditional *Guru-Shishya* model, where she taught young boys and girls free of cost.

Both my son and daughter got married eventually and got compatible life partners, who were, in the true sense, spiritual partners.

Thanks to the growth of technology, we were connected to each other, even though we were in different places most of the time, carrying on our respective work.

My Doctor continued her work in the academic field. Many students completed their PhD degrees under her guidance. Even after retiring from the university, she continued to guide the students who came to her.

My parents had grown old, but were quite healthy. With time, however, their physical activities slowed down.

In one of their regular health checkups, our family doctor said, "City life may not be good for your parents. Let them live close to nature and enjoy quietude for the rest of their lives." It made good sense for not just my parents, but also for my wife and me.

We had a big farmhouse in the outskirts of our city. It had large rooms, including my library where I enjoyed my private space.

Our family often went there for weekends. Now, we decided to reverse the routine. We moved to our farmhouse and the city house became our weekend home.

Many benefits followed. We felt like we were living in a village.

For a person like me, whose entire life had been spent in the city's hectic pace, this was a sea change. Life was slow and I had a lot of time to think and pursue creative activities.

Another advantage was that I did not have to attend to unnecessary visitors. As a successful businessman, I would get many invitations to speak, even years after my retirement.

Now, because I was living far away from the city, I always had the excuse of not being available at any phone call.

I spent my time writing more books. It did not matter to me whether or not my books became bestsellers. I enjoyed writing. I wrote because it was an expression of myself.

Also, though I did not realize it at that time, my writing was attracting a different kind of readers.

Usually, my fan club included businessmen who sought my advice on money and other business matters. Now, they were asking me spiritual questions.

I realized that my writing had changed. I had found my happiness and was guiding others to find their own true happiness. One such spiritual seeker had come to me once and said, "Sir, we would like you to speak at a conference."

Even before I could say no, I realized this young boy knew that I avoided giving lectures.

He reiterated, "Sir, please listen to me before you refuse."

# 59

# The Last Lecture

"Sir, I have read all your books and even your autobiography," he began. "I have followed you closely since my childhood. You have been my role model."

This was not at all a reason to speak at any conference. I had thousands of fans who had made me their role model.

"Sir, you represented India in Greece many years ago, when you spoke at the World Congress of Philosophy," his next statement caught my attention.

"At that time, you had spoken on Kautilya's *Arthashastra* and its relevance in management." He knew the exact details.

"Next year, the World Congress of Philosophy is being held in India. We are hosting it for the first time."

This was news to me. All the memories of going to Greece with my PhD research guide and other friends came rushing back. "Oh really, we are hosting it?" I was proud of being an Indian.

"Sir, for many years, India and its philosophy were not respected at all. You have breathed life into our culture. You not only became the richest man on earth, but your success was based on spiritual values, and you practiced the *Arthashastra* at every stage of your life."

He continued, "You became the richest man and many others followed your path of making big money in the right way. Today, India is the richest country in the world."

I was listening. His request ended with, "It would be a great message to the world, if you could be the opening keynote speaker at the World Congress of Philosophy. It will give a new direction to the world. I cannot think of a better person to represent India and its great civilization."

I thought about all my *Gurus* and mentally prayed to them. "I agree," I said, but I also told him what I felt. "It will be my last lecture."

I am not sure whether he felt happy or sad, but he got what he had come for – my acceptance.

In the next few months, everyone was surprised that I had accepted to speak after a long time. It was also publicized as my "last lecture".

This event was considered as the greatest event being hosted by our country, even bigger than hosting the Olympics or the Football World Cup. Vast crowds of scholars, religious leaders, world philosophers, community leaders and political heads from more than 180 countries assembled in India. The President and the Prime Minister of India together welcomed the world. And here I was, giving the keynote address.

I knew millions of people were watching this inaugural program live on their computers, mobiles and on the internet.

I began, "Welcome to India... the land of great sages. The land of the *Rishis*. The land of enlightenment. I stand here not just representing a country, but a civilization – the world's oldest living culture that has stood the test of time.

For many years, we have guided the world based on our spiritual values. Each person who is a seeker of the truth, from any part of the world, will get guidance from our ancient and eternal wisdom. Today, as many of you come from different parts of the world, one may ask, 'What is the Philosophy of India?' India does not have one, but many philosophies to offer.

For centuries, people from different parts of world came here to understand our philosophies. In return, we also learnt from their philosophies and their cultures. We added to our wealth of knowledge from the interaction with enlightened people from other parts of the world.

We have a culture that respects differences and accepts them as strengths, not as weaknesses. Our philosophy is enriched by various viewpoints towards the same truth. Our ancient Indian scriptures like the four Vedas, the *Mahabharata*, the *Ramayana* and the *Upanishads* are replete with discussions and debates to discover the same '*Atman*' present in each one of us.

One important point I would like to make to the world thinkers present here is that do not look at India as just a spiritual country, but also as a materially successful country. We believe that a person should be completely evolved. We need to achieve *Abhudaya* – material prosperity and *Nishrayasa* – spiritual prosperity.

The basis of material prosperity has to be *Dharma*. *Dharma* guides us at every stage of life. It is the power that keeps us together and guides each person towards the quest for truth.

I feel blessed that all my life, I have been guided by one such book on *Dharma* – Kautilya's *Arthashastra* written by Chanakya, one of the greatest philosophers of our country. He taught us that finally, happiness comes from *Dharma* – '*Sukhasya Moolam Dharma*.' I request each of you to kindly take this message of *Dharma* to your respective countries.

Once again, let us debate on and discuss the issues and concerns of the world today. Let us find philosophical answers. And let us once again guide our next generation to understand that material and spiritual prosperity are two wings of the same bird. Both wings are required for a successful flight."

I got a standing ovation. I closed my eyes and the picture of Kailash Mansarovar during my first visit came to me.

I had not just studied, but lived the *Arthashastra* in my life.

# 60

# Advice to My Grandchildren

Time takes many things away from you.

All those people whom I held close to my heart were gone from this mortal world – my parents, my *Guru* of the *Arthashastra*, my noble businessman, my chairman, various spiritual masters and my other friends.

I recollected the wisdom these people had given me. At different points in my life, they had been my guiding stars. Whenever I looked back at life, I would feel a sense of gratitude.

As the years passed by, I too was getting physically weaker, but from within, I was strong and complete. What was I waiting for – a comfortable death?

In reality, I had died long ago. The real death is not of the physical body, but of the ego. That had happened to me long ago. The body was to follow its own natural course.

When the time came, it would fall off the tree like a dried leaf. No effort would be required for the leaf to fall off. The tree will let go of the leaf on its own. I was ready to go whenever the Lord wanted me to come... nothing mattered to me at all.

My children had become parents and now I had four grandchildren. Doctor and I had settled down in a village, having enjoyed staying in the farmhouse for many years. From time to time, my kids and my grandchildren came to visit us.

Doctor and I loved to spend time with each other. They say that as you grow old, your love also matures. After many years of marriage, both of us knew each other completely. We were totally in tune with each other. Whenever we spoke, we understood each other. Most of the time, we did not need to speak at all. Silence was our method of communication too.

I spent a lot of time reading, meditating and writing books. Many material and spiritual seekers came from different parts of the world, seeking advice right from how to create wealth to how to reach God.

On their annual vacations, both our kids had come to visit us, along with their spouses and children. It was fun to have the little kids around.

One day, I was sitting in my library and my grandchildren came inside. They looked at my books and loved listening to my stories. "Grandpa, you have so many books. Have you read all of them?"

I had a hearty laugh. "Most of them, not all."

One of my granddaughters asked, "What is the best way to read a book?"

I suggested, "The best way to read a book is to understand it by studying under a *Guru*."

My grandson asked, "Grandpa, which is your favorite book among all of these?"

I was quiet. I saw myself, asking my grandfather the same question many years ago. The answer he had given me had changed my life forever.

I had nothing new to add, "Kautilya's *Arthashastra*."

It seemed that my grandchildren were smarter than me when

I asked this question. My grandson asked, "How will I benefit by studying Kautilya's *Arthashastra?*"

"Benefit?" I asked back, shocked. Then I realized that this grandson of mine had my genes, the genes of a businessman. A businessman always looks at what benefit he would get.

Even though my own children had not been keen to get into business, maybe the generation after that would continue the journey.

I had to think and give a fitting reply. As usual, the *Arthashastra* came to my rescue:

> *This science (of Arthashastra) brings into being and preserves spiritual good, material well-being and pleasures, and destroys spiritual evil, material loss and hatred. (15.1.72)*

While explaining the verse, I said, "It will free you from hatred." Finally, I said, "After you study the *Arthashastra*, something strange happens. The knowledge becomes a part of your thinking. Your thinking process becomes more evolved."

I gave this advice to my grandson. In reality, that was my final advice to all my grandchildren and all the children and youth of India.

"My grandfather had inspired me to study the Sanskrit language. I too suggest you study this great language. It is a good means of communication between you and our ancient scriptures."

Then, looking at India's development post-independence, I said, "You are a lucky generation. You do not have to struggle for survival. We are now a rich and developed nation. But do not become lazy in this prosperity. You all have work to do."

They were looking at me curiously.

"When a country becomes the richest in the world, other nations listen to it. What this country says and does will guide the world. Having become a world leader today, India and Indians have a bigger responsibility to fulfill."

I remembered all the great men and women, who had sacrificed their lives to make India great once again. "India has found its lost soul again. It is full of material and spiritual prosperity. All of you have to take that work forward."

"How do we do that?" asked my grandson.

"Study our ancient scriptures. They will guide you at every stage of your life. All of you should get inspiration from our past wisdom and work in the present for a glorious future."

My granddaughter, the youngest of the lot, asked, "Will I become smart like Chanakya then?"

"Yes, you will. You will not just become smart, but you can also help others become smart."

Smiling at her, I concluded, "It will bring out...

**The Chanakya in You..."**

# End Note

Writing has always given me immense joy. After having written two books that turned out to be bestsellers, it has given me great satisfaction as well as challenges to shoulder responsibility, as my devoted readers await another bestseller.

I then wondered what I should write next.

Fiction was something that has always fascinated me and has been close to my heart ever since I can remember. So I felt that the time had come for me to write something from a different perspective.

It has been a good many years that I have been guiding innumerable business leaders of great repute towards success and who want their progeny to also achieve indomitable success in the futures to come. It is not just these individuals but also an entire generation of young citizens who aspire to be high achievers and are seeking such wisdom to practice in their lives.

It was this thought that compelled me to weave an imaginative tale to emphasize my learnings of Kautilya's *Arthashastra* that can be applied to everyone's lives.

When the manuscript was given to my publishers, they came back with one feedback – "We can read the book at one go!" The next question they had for me was –"Is it your story?" to which I can sum up that, every book is in some way a reflection of the author's experiences.

Yes there are parts in the book that I have included from my own life. But most importantly, it includes stories from the lives of a diverse group of people I have met so far.

*Chanakya in You* is an attempt to bring to light the dreams of the young India, their frustrations and the challenges they face at every step. It is also about visionary individuals who are driven to take the country forward, to the pinnacle of prosperity.

I do hope that you enjoyed reading the book as much as I have enjoyed writing it, and also that you have connected with the stories at the deepest level, as if they were your own...

This book can be read as a work of fiction and also as one on management and life lessons that could help you as you go ahead in life. Much the way *Arthashastra* and Chanakya's wisdom continues to guide me in my journey...

**Radhakrishnan Pillai**

# About the Author

Radhakrishnan Pillai, formally educated in management and consultancy, has an MA in Sanskrit and is a certified explorer of the magic of Chanakya and the Arthashastra.

For his contributions in this field, he was honoured with the Sardar Patel International award in 2009. As the Director of SPM Foundation and a part of the University of Mumbai team, he uses the knowledge gained from his adventures to design various leadership programs. He is the founder of a spiritual tourism venture, Atma Darshan, and is also the Founder-Director of the Chanakya Institute of Public Leadership (www. ciplmumbai.in), a leadership academy which trains political leaders and aspirants. After the runaway success of his first book *Corporate Chanakya*, followed by a second bestseller *Chanakya's 7 Secrets of Leadership*, Radhakrishnan Pillai brings Chanakya to life in his business fiction *Chanakya in You*.

# Index for Chapters